From The Pit
To The Palace

To all who have been abused
physically, emotionally, mentally and sexually
but work to overcome hardship

From The Pit
To The Palace

Written By
Tiffany McIntosh

Illustration By
Aya Asar

Cover Designed By
Sun Child Wind Spirit

Proofread By
Calvin McIntosh

Edited By
Mylia Tiye Mal Jaza

From the Pit to the Palace (vol 1)

Paperback ISBN-13: 978-1689006705
Hardcover ISBN-13: 978-0-359-94550-4

Author
Tiffany McIntosh
www.TiffanyMcIntosh.webs.com

Self-Publishing Associate
Dr. Mary M. Jefferson
BePublished.Org - Chicago, IL
(972) 880-8316
www.bepublished.org

First Edition. Printed In the USA
Recycled Paper Encouraged.

Table of Content

◆

(MORE)

TOC *continued*

CHAPTER 1
Little Girl Lost

When I was a child, I lived with Family Members That were mental abusers. They would always tell me what I couldn't do and speak all kinds of defeat over my life.

"You gone have a bunch of kids. You ain't gone have no husband."

I can remember other people telling me I couldn't do things and I would end up doing it, or they would say I would do bad things and I never did do. No, I don't have a house full of kids. No, I'm not on welfare. No, I don't live in the projects. No to a whole bunch of stuff that I heard that people tried to drop in my spirit growing up. None of those things they tried to curse me with are the case in my life at all. Let me go back a little farther and come forward for you from there.

I was a lost little girl. My dad was in and out of my life. I knew who he was growing up and saw him periodically. He was in and out of jail, went from selling drugs to doing drugs, and delivered me a lot of broken promises. So, my mom met a guy and he became my youngest brother's father and my stepdad. We kind of moved around a lot because he was a long-distance truck driver. That was why I started to love traveling so much, because he let us see the world in his 18-wheeler. We lived everywhere. Georgia, Florida, Alabama. You name it.

Our final stop was Tulsa, Oklahoma. Shortly After moving there my great aunt Lori (my grandmother's sister) Was Diagnosed With Breast Cancer. She didn't have any children, and she's actually the person who named me. She almost died when I was 10 years old. . She was staying at the Cancer Treatment Center of America. Her husband stayed back in Cleveland, Ohio, because he still had to work. He would fly out periodically and see her.

Once she got released, when they said she was well enough to go home, I actually went back to Ohio with her to help her. I was happy helping her, but we know it's one thing to help family and it's another thing to be with your own parents. I really wanted to go back home with my mom. But, I stayed there helping my great aunt for a year and then went back to Tulsa with my mom.

By the time I got back, I was 11 and she was a single mom working two jobs. My stepdad she was with when I left was no longer in the picture. He had been cheating on my mom with her best friend, who was the neighbor next door. Mom had met someone else though, and they were kind of dating. I was the one that stayed at home with my brothers after school, even though I was just 11. We didn't know anybody there and we didn't have any family there. Mom just kind of met people along the way. A young lady named Sheila that she met who lived in the same projects we lived in had a daughter and three sons. Her oldest son Keon started watching us, babysitting while they were working, because his mom and our mom worked together. He was 17.So One Day While Watching Us He Came On To Me. He Assured Me It Was Ok! He Wanted To Show Me How To Be A Woman. This Is The Day I lost my Innocence. He took my virginity.

I didn't know what was going on. I was scared. I was bleeding and I didn't know what to tell mom. At the same time, I didn't know how to tell her. I knew what happened wasn't good and wasn't right. I didn't feel good. I felt dirty. I felt like I should have been outside playing with my friends. I was just lost.

This happened to me for about a year until my mom found out about it. I finally told her. I think that was a turning point in my life. I started to feel inadequate. I felt responsible even though I was just 11. *How could I let this happen?* I felt I was responsible for it happening to me even though I was just A kid. I didn't feel good about myself. I went through a lot of emotional things.

My whole life, I battled with my weight. I felt like I just existed, like people just looked over me. At this time, I didn't get a chance to see a lot of my mom. As we know, as parents, we have to do what we gotta do to make things happen. We gotta go out here and work to be able to survive to make sure our kids can eat. I was a little girl lost because I had a lot of grown up responsibilities although I was only a little girl.

CHAPTER 2
Burdened & Abused

When I talked to my mom about everything again, she actually exploded. She flipped out on me. That really caused some issued between us. I don't know if she was angry at the fact that the act happened or that I didn't tell her when it first happened. Communication has always been a struggle. I think that became the pinnacle of me looking for love in all the wrong places.

I'm 12 years old by now, and my mom had gotten a better job. She was a supervisor at a Nascar Plant. Not only was I really looking for a mom, I was looking for love from a man.

My new stepfather, who had come into her life and really raised me from that point, was the best thing that could have happened to my mom. He came into her life, worked for the City of Tulsa for just as long as I've been alive now, and we moved out of those projects and in a really nice home with him. We didn't really do a lot of things. Our parents were working so we were usually just going to school and coming home, and I would be the one babysitting my brothers (one four years younger than me and one six years younger than me). I was cleaning, cooking , doing laundry, and all of that stuff I'd been doing since I was 11. I was the one responsible for doing things during those times mom was working two jobs.

But like I said, at that point, I was looking for love. I was looking for acceptance. I was looking for a lot of different things. One day I was out, met some kids and kind of got into the wrong crowd. Like I said, looking for acceptance. We moved to a good neighborhood and started going to a good school.

One day, I was hanging with some of the new friends I had met, and I met this guy named Chris. At this time, I was 13 and Chris was 18. Chris was handsome, popular, and was giving me attention and did I Say Bad Boy .Chris was part of a gang, the Crips. Now, I had gotten acceptance from this group. *I'm with these bad boys.* They're toting guns, breaking in cars, and doing all kinds of stuff.

My mom was still always working. Since they started a summer program at McDonald's, I started working at McDonald's at 13. She got a work permit from my school and I started working there. My friends would come up to my job periodically, and so would Chris. He and his friends started coming to my job all the time. This one particular day, a young lady named Nae I had already befriended was with them in a different car and they asked me to chill when I got off work.

"You should come with us when you get off work."

I told them I was getting off in 30 minutes, at 7 p.m., so they stayed and ate. Instead of me walking home when I got off work, I called my mom and told her I was going over to Nae's house and then I would come home.

"Make sure you come home by your curfew," she told me.

I said, "Okay."

CHAPTER 3
Tough Though Trampled

We hung up and I got in the car with my crew and just started hanging out with them. I wanted to be around Chris. He was older, he was attractive, and he was popular. We went joyriding, went out to eat, and did all kinds of things. When it started getting dark, we started making our way to my house. As we got to a particular neighborhood not too far from where I lived, time we hit the corner, a police officer hit the corner and got behind us.

I didn't think anything of it until the boy driving said, "Shoot! The police are behind us."

The next thing I knew, the police lights came on and Chris's friend hit the gas. He took the police on a high-speed chase through a well-known, upper class neighborhood. Come to find out, the car was stolen. I didn't know that. But before we knew it, we were in an accident. His friend had lost control of the car, ran up in somebody's yard, knocked their mailbox down, hit a tree, and spun the car into their garage. Their whole garage was bent in. The guys jumped out of the car, so I jumped out of the car because I was on the back seat.

Chris grabbed my hand and was like, "Run! Let's go! know the neighborhood like that." We hopped a fence and got separated. We wound up in an apartment complex. So, I knocked on this lady's door and told her I was in trouble. I said, "Can I use her phone to call my mom?"

So, she let me come in to call my mom and told my mom to come get me. I was crying and I was shaking. I told her what apartment I would be at.

"Oh, I'll tell you what's going on later. I just need you to come get me."

So, she said, "Okay, I'm on my way."

Then, I gave her the lady's address. As I hung up, the lady expressed her concern.

"Are you okay, honey?" The lady asked.

She didn't know it was the police chasing me. She figured somebody else chasing me, like somebody trying to kill me or something. She was very kind and helped calm me from my panicky state. As I'm waiting on my mom, I hear people's doors getting knocked on. At this point, I knew it was the police knocking on people's doors.

So, I told the lady, "Well, I'm gonna go out the backdoor cause my mom said she was gonna pick me up on the other side. Thank you for letting me use your phone."

I went out the back door. I rounded the building. I heard a click, click. It was them cocking their guns back. They told me I better not move or they would blow my head off.

Needless to say, my mama never picked me up from the lady's house. She picked me up from the detention center. And, she

16

was pissed! She picked me up from there and I had to go through a special program and all of that stuff. But I still talked to Chris. He was, like I said, just everything. With him, I ended up involved in all kinds of shoot-outs. Then, after that he required more of me.

He was like, "Okay, well, if you want to be with me, then you gone have to get initiated into our gang."

At 14, that's what I did. I got initiated into their gang. I was riding around with them and breaking into houses. We were just doing all kinds of stuff. one day when me and my mom got into it about something, I ran away with Chris. I think I was gone from home for four months and was staying at his mom's house and different houses that the gangs had. We were doing stuff with them and getting into trouble. I mean, I wasn't getting in trouble but was just doing stuff that could get us in trouble. You know, breaking into folks' places and just doing all this stuff that was definitely not my character. But like I said, I just wanted the acceptance.

CHAPTER 4
Making Mad Moves

I thought he loved me. I felt like he loved me. So, I loved him. Once again, he's way older than me. At this time, I'm 14 and that means he's 19, getting ready to be 20. I'm with him every day, running the streets and doing some of everything. Then, one day I got sick, I mean really sick. I was throwing up And was having really bad abdominal pain and they had to take me to the Emergency Room. The physicians wouldn't treat me because they didn't have the consent of my mom. So, they called her to get consent to treat! My mom already had a Missing Person's Report out on me because she couldn't find me. She didn't know where I was. All she knew was I had run away with Chris. She didn't know where we were.

Right before that trip to the emergency room, they had broken into somebody's house and they went in there and got some petty stuff. I told him I didn't want to go.

"I'll stay," I told him because I knew even then that wasn't supposed to be my life. "I don't wanna go."

I guess the guy didn't get everything he went in to get and that was the first time that ever happened. The guy Chris was with made it my fault that they didn't get everything that they wanted. Chris jumped on me. That was the first time, but he beat me badly. He blacked my eye and busted my lips. I was completely caught off guard. He was smacking me, kicking me, everything. Soon, this became regular.

About the third or fourth time he did it, I fought back. Because, what you not going to do is keep whooping on me every time something doesn't go your way

That's how my mom initially found me. She called the police and told them that the hospital had called her, and she was on her way there and could they meet her there. When Chris saw the police come in, he left.

"I don't know if I'm going to jail for keeping you with me this long, or what's going to happen," he said.

So, he left. I was just in there by myself, hooked up to an IV. They were running all kinds of tests on me, trying to see if I had a urinary tract infection and all of that kind of stuff. Well, I had a UTI, but I was also six weeks pregnant. Now, I'm in the eighth grade and pregnant with a baby. I'm going to school and doing everything I'm supposed to do after my mom gets me back. I stopped talking to Chris for a minute and then he came back into my life.

He was like, "Look, if you have this baby, I am going to be here for my baby. I promise I ain't gone hit you no more."

You know how abusers do. They always tell you everything you want to hear exactly when you want to hear it. But, I wasn't doing none of the crazy stuff like breaking in houses. None of that was still going on. Anyway, I went to school one day and during lunch I kept feeling a bad pain in my back. I was about four months pregnant at the time. Back then, there were no cell phones all around like they are now. So, it wasn't like I could text my mom.

I went to the school nurse and told her what was going on. After I finished telling her everything I was feeling, and how the pain was in my back, she had me to call my mom at work but Before my mom could get to the school to pick me up, I started having really bad cramps. They had to call the paramedics because my water broke at school in the nurse's office. My mom was coming to the school from her job, which was almost an hour away.

"We need to get her some medical attention now," the nurse called back and told my mother. "Just meet us at the hospital."

She met us at the hospital. I was in full-blown labor at that moment. So, I called Chris's mom and told his mom what was happening. Wherever he was at, she went and got him and they came to the hospital. I wound up having a stillborn baby. I named her Tia Janae. Even though I was young, I was feeling like this was going to be my baby and I would have someone who would give me unconditional love. I felt like, if nobody shows me love, I know she will. *Even if I'm not with Chris*

When I lost her, I just went through a horrible, horrible, horrible depression. I thought about suicide a lot. One day, I tried to kill myself. I'm glad that it did not work. When I look back over it, that's definitely the worst depression I ever went through.

Because I just kept saying, "I don't want to be here," and I just wanted to take my own life, they kept me for evaluation. I stayed there for about two weeks. Once they released me, I left my mom's house again and went back to Chris. I was with him for maybe two weeks. While I was with him, he had gotten into it with a rival gang really, really bad. We weren't on the side of town where we lived. We were on the opposite side of town and were waiting at the traffic light to jump on the expressway. Just as the light turned and we pulled off and started to merge onto the expressway, the guys started shooting at us and Chris popped back.

So, we had a full-blown shootout while we were driving on the freeway and they were riding on the side street. These guys were Bloods. They had already been having a back-and-forth feud and been into it with Chris. That particular day was the first time in a long time that they had run back into Chris.

It was Chris, me, another young lady Sarah, and Sarah's boyfriend riding together. When the Bloods started shooting, we'd gotten on the ramp and they kept shooting as they rode the past. As we were coming up on that ramp, they were still shooting and Chris popped back a few rounds here and there as he punched the gas, jetting past the vehicles that seemed oblivious to us and forced him to keep changing lanes. This was a full-blown shootout at two o'clock in the afternoon on the expressway!

That's why I be so thankful when I just think about what all God has brought me through. At that moment, I made a decision. That night, I stayed with him. Then, after that, I was like, "I'm good." *I'm over it. I don't want it. I'm cool. I'm cool on him. It's not worth it. Yeah. This, this is just too much.* See, one thing about gangs is once they think you are a threat, they don't care if you are a girl or boy. They will kill your mama and them. I had to make some changes happen to protect my family.

I wound up, the next day, having him take me home. He took me home to my mom's house and I just told my mom what my plans were, what I wanted to do. She couldn't stand Chris, of course, so she was glad that I had decided to get away from him. In the neighborhood where my mom lived, things were nice. We lived in a good neighborhood and everybody knew everybody. So, my friends were excited I was back. This one friend was dating a guy who lived on the next street over from us.

She said, "Come over here and walk around here with me."

Now, mind you, it's summertime and it's more than 100 degrees outside. I got on a dress, a long maxi dress, and some shoes. They had a little heel on them. We get to this boy's house, and the boy has a friend up there. My friend called herself trying to hook us up.

"Like, I'm not talking to none of his friends, but I will be cordial," I told her.

So, while she's talking to her boyfriend, we're all standing out there in the front yard. Next thing I know, a white car comes around the corner. I didn't know whose car it was, but the car caught all our attention the way it came around the corner. *Hmm,* I was thinking, *this gotta be somebody who doesn't live in this neighborhood driving like this.* When the white car gets closer, I see it's the dudes Chris had the shootout with. They instantly opened fire on me. My friend and the two guys we were standing out front with ran in the house and locked the door.

Mind you, I didn't go nowhere without a gun. I pulled out my gun and started shooting back. As I ran, I had to kick off my shoes and hold up my dress so I wouldn't be slowed up or risk falling. They're still shooting at me and I'm still shooting at them. Remember how I told you it was really hot outside that day. I understated it. The pavement was so hot, it burned the soles of my feet as I ran for my life that day.

I ran, ran, ran. It was a restaurant called Perkins that I saw through the trees after jumping some fences and everything to get away from that car. I ran to Perkins and banged on the back door. I told them that somebody was trying to kill me. The manager let me in, and I called my mother.

My feet were bleeding. The pavement was so hot as I ran that day that I literally had holes that looked like craters in the bottom of my feet.

When my mother came up there and got me, she said, "You're going back to Ohio. I'm going to send you to live with your grandmother now."

Mind you, this is my dad's mom she was referring to. I knew of them, but I didn't know them like that. I would see them during visits periodically when I was smaller, but I didn't know them well enough to feel comfortable living with them. I expressed this to my mother.

Mama said, "I would rather send you to live with them than for them to call me and tell me I gotta bury you."

So, she called my aunt Kacey – my dad's sister And said I'm scared for her life! At that time, my aunt was living with my grandmother. She had just got on the police force. Well, she had been on there for a couple of years, but she was living with my grandma because she was having a house built. My aunt told my mom to send me there and my staying with her would be no problem.

"Oh, yes! Send her. She can stay here. We don't want nothing to happen to her. Send her here so she could stay here and, when my house gets done getting built-out, I'll take her with me. But, right now, we all have to stay here at Mama while they're building my house," I could hear my aunt saying through the receiver as I sat across from my mother.

My mom told my aunt that would be the plan and she looked at me and said, "Okay."

The next day, she packed my bags and got me a ticket to Ohio. The day she put me on that plane was life-altering, but not in the way she hoped. It led to one of the worst experiences I ever had with family and in life ever. When she put me on that plane, it was with the thought that I would be better off . However, I landed into a big mess. When my aunt's house was finished being built, she moved out. I was sad I didn't go with her.

All I could think was, *I'm really on my own now!* I was already pretty much fending for myself. My grandmother already had custody of my cousin. He was a straight menace to society. Both my dad and my uncle were in and out of jail and prison. They both were on and off drugs, you know. Her house was one where everyone stayed so you had to lock your stuff up because you don't want it to come up missing and be for sale.

That was how I met the father of my middle daughter. Since I had worked at McDonald's in Oklahoma, I altered my birth certificate so I could get a job in Ohio. Why? Because my grandmother let me live there but she provided limited things. Basically, she got a check for me, but she didn't get much for me. My mom would send me new shoes once and month. Whatever else I needed, I had to provide it for myself.

"Mom, she says hurtful things," I explained to my mother.

She would call me fat. She'd say things like, "Ain't no man gone want you. You gone wind up with a bunch of babies who gonna live in the projects. You ain't gone do nothing with your life!"

Where did that come from? Why would someone talk to your own grandchild child like that? Of course, my mom didn't know anything about this prior to my telling her because she didn't know them intimately like that. All she thought she was doing was getting me out of a bad place to a better one. She was hurt to hear that I was being talked to like that, and she encouraged me to keep working and being wise with my money that summer.

At the time I'm sharing a room with my little cousin. I was getting ready to go into the 9th Grade and my aunt did take me to get a couple of things! and going to high school with everything I needed, although I was tired a lot of days but still got my homework done. I was proud of myself.

CHAPTER 5
Stepping In Quicksand

The year after that, my uncle came home from jail after getting into trouble. He had full reign of the house and zero accountability or responsibility. Needless to say, he quickly got back on drugs. I knew, being 15, I would have to start securing my personal belongings better than I had been doing before my uncle came back home. Everybody in the house knew what we were facing. He was on and off drugs, in and out of the house.

As you know, I was already used to fending for myself and had the job at McDonald's . I knew they did their best to provide, but my needs increased. So, I got a second job when school was out and worked them both over the summer. I work at McDonald's and I worked at this place called Bunny's. It was a barbecue carryout place. The crazy part about it though is sometimes I would get off from Bunny's at 11 o'clock at night and I would have to walk home even though it was stark dark outside. I felt like I didn't have a life, so I called my mom crying. She also reminded me of the big picture and the main reason she sent me there.

"There's nothing I can really do about it. We know I can't have you come back here," she candidly expressed.

I was making just enough with the two jobs at that time to pay for my basic necessities. It wasn't enough to stay by myself, but it was enough to buy myself school clothes. Throughout the summer, all I was doing was stocking up on clothes for school. Once I got paid from one job, I go somewhere and buy me an outfit or two, and then I put it in my closet. And when I got paid from my other job, I'd buy another outfit or two and put it in the closet. That way, when school started, it would be like I had a bunch of stuff. Plus, that made it to where, if my grandmother did do anything for me with the check she got from me being there, it would be in addition to what I was already doing for myself.

Thankfully, all my cousins went to the same school I did when the school year started. My mom's family lived there in Akron too. My cousins, in my mind, were a reminder that I had family too. Seeing them made me feel like I was good with my family. After school started, my cousins and I were having a lot of fun. We were reconnecting and doing stuff together, so I felt a lot better.

But at the same time, like I have admitted already, I had a lot of responsibilities at 15. So, one day my friends at school were having a party. A couple of them were older than me, and some of them were like 16. Some of their parents had bought them their first cars already. They all had card and I did not. This particular weekend of my friend's party was back when they had pagers out.

I was like, *All I do is work and go to school. I'm going to that party.* I never really knew what it was to be a teenager at that point. My friend said she would come and pick me up. All I had to do was send her a page when I was almost ready. The plan was, by the time she got there, I'll be ready to walk out the door. But, I had to work.

"I'm gonna go home and take me a shower, and you can get me from the house," I told her.

. When I got off and got back home, I took my shower. As I started getting dressed, I paged my friend. So, I thought. The house phone rings, and I heard somebody on the other end of the phone who wasn't my girl.

"Yeah, somebody paged me," the real deep voice said.

"I paged somebody, but I don't think that I was supposed to be paging you," I confessed.

Still, I was curious. I knew I had paged Asia. He must have her pager or something.

"Who is this?" I asked.

"This TD," he said.

"Oh, I must have dialed the wrong pager number," I said.

He told me his number. I realized what happened. I'd dialed the wrong number for sure. His was one digit off from my friend's number. I immediately thought to call my friend to tell her to be on her way, but the thought slipped my mind as TD and I kept talking. I wound up not going to the party period. He kept me on the phone forever. I didn't even care that TD kept me on the phone. I was happy to have met him.

As time passed, we weren't just talking here and there but we were talking every single day. I would also talk to him when I got home after work. Now, at this time, I'm still 15 and he was 20. So, one day I'm working both my jobs and I get off and I'm scared to walk home because I stayed later than normal. By the time we got done cleaning up, it was 12 o'clock. *I don't want to walk these dark streets by myself.* Now mind you, I'd been talking to TD on the phone for four months at this point. We'd never seen each other.

All we had done was talked on the phone and I'd tell him about my day, about my problems, and about how I hated my life. He would get so mad, although we had never met face-to-face.

Anyway, this particular day, I got up the nerve and I said, "Can you come get me?"

TD said, "Where are you?"

I said, "I'm just now getting off of work. I was supposed to get off at 10, but I stayed over and I helped them clean up. Now, I'm too scared to walk home at this time of night by myself."

He was like, "I'm on my way."

And, he came. Yup. And that's how we met. Even though we had been talking on the phone for months, we never physically met in person until that day. He picked me up, and from that moment we were inseparable. He was picking me up from school, taking me to work, and taking me out. Everybody was in awe at my high school.

"Is that her dude?"

"Her dude got a car!"

"They be everywhere together."

But the crazy part about it was the fact that they all assumed we were sleeping together, and we had never had sex. I liked how we did what we did. *This is cool.* I was hanging out with him at their house and hanging out with him at his spot. See, he was a d-boy, but you wouldn't have ever known it. TD was very low-key, very humble, very behind the scenes. He wasn't flashy or nothing. He was very quiet, very meticulous, very laid back, very mellow. He was, just everything. We were together every day.

Well, until one day he was supposed to come pick me up. But, it never happened. It took a while for me to realize TD wasn't going to show up. *What's going on? What happened? Where is he?* I started blowing up his pager. He wasn't calling me back. I knew something wasn't right. I called his mom and she told me that TD had been arrested. I assumed he had gotten pulled over on his way to get me. I felt guilty.

Guessing he got pulled over, I knew he must have had some drugs in the car in order to get arrested. He had never been in trouble before they arrested him that day. He was going back and forth to court for months. The day finally came that we were looking forward to, his final court date.

"Take this just in case I don't come back up out of here," TD said.

"Don't talk like that," I told him, pushing the envelope back into his hands. "They're gonna give you probation cause you ain't

31

never been in no trouble before, you know. Hell, you ain't even had a speeding ticket."

So, we went down to his courtroom and waited for his case to be called. They get going and, of course, he has a court-appointed attorney. His first-time offense, they sentenced him to two years in prison that day. In the courtroom, they let him give me his pager and all his stuff, including his jewelry and $8,000 in cash.

"Take care of you with this. I'm gonna be alright. I'll call my mom and have my mom call you," he said.

He honored his word too. That happened for a few months. Then, one day while I was at work, my uncle that was living back with us wreaked havoc. You already know he was on drugs really bad. Because he was living at grandma's, I had to put a padlock on my bedroom door and everything because you don't never know what he might do or when. Though I padded up my room, I come home from work and the padlock was off the door.

"It's some mess in this game," I couldn't help but acknowledge.

He had beat the lock off my door while I was at work. You already know I immediately went through the house and started looking for him after coming out of my room. While I'm going through my room, all of my clothes and valuables are gone, and stuff is all over the place. Everything I had been buying for school was gone. After I didn't find him anywhere in the house, I realized that this cat done stole everything and went to go sell it.

I'm up there crying. I go in and tell my grandma. But, I go in and tell her what my uncle, did to me.

"I can't believe he stole my stuff," I'm telling her with tears flowing. "He beat off my padlock, took my stuff, and everybody's pretending like they didn't see or hear anything!"

My grandmother was unphased. The only emotion she showed when it did come out was anger directed at me. She basically acted like I was lying on her son. Then, her attitude switched to one asking what I want her to do before she really got ugly with me.

"You know he has a problem. How do you know it was him?" Were some of the comments she made.

My uncle was gone for like two days. On day number three, he shows his face because now that money has run out. I'm upstairs and I had just gotten dressed. When he gets near the top of the stairs, I'm standing at the top. We got to arguing. We got into it really bad about my stuff.

"I know you stole it! I worked for my stuff," I told my uncle.

He said something out of his neck to me and I snapped. We got to arguing like two adults as he stepped on the top of the staircase in front of me. My grandmother was in her room, the next room over, and she came out yelling.

"Don't be talking to him like that. Who do you think you are? Then my uncle chimed in, "If it's anything in here I want, I will take it anytime! I will take it!"

What did he say that to me for? Baby! I snapped and hauled off and punched him. I was 15 about to be 16, and my uncle was around 34 or 35. We were fighting like two grown men in my grandmother's house. We fell down the stairs and everything, but I was still fighting all the way to the living room with him. I tore up her living room with him and tried to throw him through the window at one point.

The next thing I knew, my grandmother was yelling at me, "Get your stuff and out of my house!"

She told me that. He was in his 30s and 19 years older than me, but I was the one she saw was wrong. Looking back, I understand that his being her child and her oldest son made him especially special to her (if anyone could be). Once again, I called my mom.

"Mom, she told me get out after I confronted him about stealing my stuff and he and I got into a fight," I explained. Ma remembered our family friend, a friend of our family that's like my auntie to me. Ma reminded me that my god aunt lives maybe about 8-9 minutes from my grandma's house. So, I got a bag and I walked to my god aunt's house. Upon arrival, she took me back up to my grandma's house to get the rest of my stuff because I couldn't carry it all.

She allowed me to stay at her place for an undetermined amount of time. My staying there helped me and worked out for her because she kind of needed a babysitter. She had a lot she was doing, and she also loved to party. I told her that, while I'm there, I'm able to babysit for her when I was off work. That way, when she went out to parties, I would be at the house with the kids watching movies and getting them ready for bed. Things were rolling smoothly for about a month or two.

Then, one of her cousins from her dad's people moved there with her. I kept telling her that he made me feel uncomfortable because he was an alcoholic. I mean, full blown. Anytime somebody gets up getting drunk at nine o'clock in the morning, it's a problem. When my god aunt would go out, he would go out with her. Often, he brought people back to the house with them, mostly girls. This wasn't a problem really because, like I said, I would be the babysitter. I even babysat for one of her friends who went out with her and paid me to watch her kids.

One evening when they got back around two or three o'clock in the morning, apparently my god aunt and her boyfriend went into her room as her friend got her kids, who had fallen asleep like the rest of the kids and me. Me and the kids had gone to bed early, about 11 or 11:30. I was in my room upstairs in the bed knocked out. Then, I kept feeling something pulling on me. I opened my eyes. I caught my god aunt's cousin fondling me

Am I tripping? What the hell? I was half asleep and half awake, and I didn't know if this was real or not. Then, I felt him put his hand over my mouth. I knew this was real and was now fully awake. I started looking around and I looked at him. I kept looking at him. I mumbled his name.

"Donald?" I said has his had covered my mouth.

"Shut up," he exclaimed in a whisper.

He started pulling down my underwear with his free hand. We started tussling as I tried to free myself from him. That was probably the worst day of my life. I know it's hard to conceptualize, considering what I told you already. But, believe me, it was the worst day ever for me. At that time, Donald had to have been about 23 or 24 and I was still 15. Um, we know what happened from there. Right? I can't go into all the things he did to me. Just know, he continued violated me despite my protest.

I wasn't going to be victimized in silence like he'd hoped. He didn't know me. We literally went from tussling to brawling. After that all happened, I was looking like somebody from "Amistad." I mean, when I say I looked like somebody else, that wouldn't begin to summarize it. I'll just say, they had to take me to the hospital. I was bleeding from some of everywhere, my mouth was busted. I was even bleeding out of my eyes.

When I was taken to the emergency room and my aunt came in there, she didn't even recognize me. She walked right past my room. She looked at me, walked past my room, and didn't recognize me.

She went to the desk and asked, "What room is she in?"

That was very traumatic for me. My mom's mom worked for Child Protective Services at that time. I wound up moving in with my once that happened. Afterwards, we had court proceedings. I had to go through CSB, and I had to get counseling. I had to go through all kinds stuff. And, like I said my grandmother worked for children's services, so I couldn't skip any of the steps no matter how much I protested. At first, I didn't want the counseling. I really didn't want to talk about what Donald did to me and all the other things I'd been through prior to that. I just wanted to bury everything.

Once they released me from the hospital, I went home with my grandma and she went over to my god aunt's house to get my stuff. Remember now, our families were really close. Their family was like my family before I was even born. Like my aunt and the lady whose house I was at, they all grew up telling people they were cousins. People generally thought they were real cousins. But after I got from the hospital, I had to talk to the police. That drove a wedge between the two families.

CHAPTER 6
Difficulty Bears A Gift

So, after that happened over the summer, and school started, I was 16. I couldn't believe what I had gone through and wanted to live my life like I was normal. They started school right after Labor Day. I was in the 10th grade. Since I went to school with my cousins, I felt comfortable enough to start getting involved in things and just trying to get my life back because that really broke me right there. I was really broken. Donald broke me to the core.

One of my girl cousins was like, "It's not your fault."

But I was still asking, "Why all this bad stuff gotta keep happening to me?"

She and I just kinda grew a really, really close bond. We were more like sisters than cousins.. She was, more so, helping me get through within because I didn't want to go to counseling. One day when we were at school, it was our pep rally day. During the pep rally, everybody was trying to see which grade was going to be the loudest during the cheer contest and who was going to do this and that.

We sat at the top of the bleachers. We were up there screaming the year that we would graduate. We were supposed to graduate in 1998. This was in 1996 and we yelled, "98" as loud as we could when it was our turn to represent. All of my girl cousins and all my good girlfriends – were up there screaming because we all graduated the same year. The next thing I knew, I woke up in the back of an ambulance.

The last thing I remembered was being up at the top of the bleachers screaming, "98" and then seeing things slow down and fade to black. It really was like in a movie, or like maybe somebody drugged me or something. Everything started to go really slow and I went down. Thank God some of my friends and my cousins went to high school with me. All of my crew, they said, rushed to my aide.

They said I fell down the bleachers after losing my balance. The doctors said the imbalance was due to something occurring in my body based on how I described the slow motion and fading out. Of course, I was being treated at the children's hospital again, and they ran a lot of tests on me. They checked my blood sugar to make sure that it was on point and they were checking my blood pressure to make sure I didn't have a drop in pressure.

"Periodically, that can happen to people when their blood pressure drops. They're known to pass out," the physician said when explaining the reasons for the tests.

After a while, they came in and said I was three and a half months pregnant. They said that was why my equilibrium was off. I mentally checked out at that point. I hadn't been doing anything since TD went to prison, so I knew whose baby it was. Donald's rape wouldn't seem to go away. I had to find a way to deal with it, permanently.

I went through this battle with myself. *Lord, do I still have it and give it away? Do I have an abortion and kill a baby? Do I keep the baby?* It was a mental battle for weeks. That's why me and my son's relationship is so tight. We have a different kind of relationship because he knows the whole truth. He knows his family and has met his other siblings through his father. There's another young lady that's his sister and her mom said Donald did the same thing to her. He met them right before we moved to Texas two years ago.

But while I was going through the pregnancy, I tried hard not to miss a beat and come to terms with everything. That was when I accepted that I really did need any kind of help I could get. I just couldn't believe it. *It can't be. This can't be right, not with what this came from.* I was asking myself things like: *How do you have a baby with somebody that did this to you? I don't want my son or my daughter to have to know about this.* Being pregnant was just physically draining and mentally challenging with this back and forth. *Like, Do I keep him, or do I not keep him?*

The ladies were like, "If you're going to get the abortion, you have to get it before 20 weeks."

I knew then that I couldn't do it. But, I kept saying to myself that I'll go back and get it done. I didn't want the memory. I didn't want the stigma. I didn't want to pass on his genes. I didn't want to kill a baby. I didn't want to deny a life. So, I went through that for so long that my brief four weeks were past, and I couldn't have an abortion even if I wanted to. In a way, that helped relieve a lot of pressure. I took a deep breath that day as I left the abortion clinic. Sitting and waiting for the bus, I took time to analyze my situation. *How do I feel about Donald? How do I feel about TD?* I mean, he wasn't going to be in jail forever. *So, like, how do I do this? How do I tell him what Donald did to me? I really don't want to take him through this.*

After all, TD was the one person who was always down for me. He was amazing. He was the only person I felt loved me and genuinely loved me. He looked out for me. Nobody else ever looked out for me. It crushed my heart to watch him go to jail. It melted it when he gave me that $8,000 before they took him away and he told me to take care of myself with it while he was gone. *How do I tell him about what happened?*

I'm at my grandma's house, just sitting outside on the porch of course, and she was in the kitchen cooking. It was smelling good too. The phone rang and I ran inside to answer it. I didn't want nothing to pull my grandma from the kitchen. When I answered, I was glad I did. It was TD's sister on the other end of the phone.

"Hey! How you doing?" She greeted.

Mind you, I ain't seen none of them since any of this stuff with Donald happened. First of all, I wasn't going to be able to go around them because I didn't feel comfortable telling them nothing before I told TD.

"Hey, girl. What's been going on?" I responded.

She was like, "Yo, where you been?"

41

I told her my work schedule.

"You always be working," she said.

I was like, "Yep. I'm always working.

. Then, she started talking about how they never see me.

"Wait, hold on a minute," she said. I have somebody that wants to talk to you."

She patched TD in on three-way. I could not believe it. I was so happy and so sad at the same time. I started crying on the phone.

He was like, "What's up, boo?"

I was like, "Hey."

And he goes, "What's going on? I miss you. I was sitting there thinking about how I was eight months pregnant. I felt so guilty. I was feeling isolated. I was feeling a whole bunch of things. I was feeling confusion. But, he and I talked on the phone for 30 minutes.

I said, "How are we able to talk this long? We've been on the phone for 30 minutes, and we normally can only talk for 15."

I wondered how we were able to be on the phone all that time and the people hadn't come on and said we had one minute left. He told me that he was in a halfway house and was about to finish his sentence.

"I'm actually in Akron now at the halfway home," TD said. "I had my sister call you. I'm gonna give you this number so you can call me back on the pay phone. I want you to call me back time we get off."

I consented, jotted the number, and called him back after thanking Keila for calling me. It really meant a lot to me that she made it happen for us. I couldn't let her hang up without expressing my appreciation.

"Thank you, Keila," I told her.

So, she was like, "You're welcome."

I immediately called him back on the pay phone. TD had been gone for nine months and what happened with Donald happened a couple of weeks after TD left. This was like a good month after. I made it a point to tell him everything during that first call we had without someone else on the line, but it wouldn't come out easily, and I told him how school was getting ready to start for me.

We kept talking and talking. I couldn't bring myself to tell him. I couldn't steal joy from him like that. I knew I wanted to see him but that I couldn't let him see me without telling him about my pregnancy first.

"Why don't you come down to the halfway house and see me? I could put you down on my visitation list," he said.

But I wasn't ready to let him see me. I still hadn't told him what happened yet.

"I'm coming down there. But, don't you get out on a pass," I said.

"Yeah, but I gotta stay here for 30 days first," he said.

"Okay. I'll see what I can do," I told him.

This was me just talking. We kept talking every day for maybe three days. Then, I suddenly busted out crying.

"What's wrong? Why are you crying? What's going on?" He inquired.

Now, the day before, I didn't know if he had heard something and was suspicious or what. But, he was saying how his family was saying they hadn't seen me since shortly after he went to prison.

"They say you been gone," he said.

"No. I have to deal with school, work and all this other stuff," I told him.

In truth, since Donald raped me a couple of weeks after TD went in, I had not been really going around nobody unless it was at school or work. "I need to tell you something. We need to seriously talk," I told TD.

Then I told him about what happened to me. After that, I told him that I needed to tell him something else.

"What?" He asked, trying to contain his anger.

"I got pregnant," I said.

We sat in silence on the phone for a few seconds.

"What's this dude's name and what does he look like? From the situation, I want to kill him," TD said.

Then, after talking about how crazy he would go on Donald, TD finally calmed down.

"I'm sorry. I'm sorry you went through that," he said. "Tell you what. That sucka don't even matter no more. You tell me. What are we having?"

I could hear the smile in his voice. I really started crying.

I told him, "It's a boy."

He said, "So, that's why you haven't been around my people?"

I told him, "Yeah," and he surprised me again.

"I've been gone for nine months. They don't know if that's my baby or not," he said.

He didn't want me to tell them, but I wanted them to know. At first, TD wouldn't tell his family that my son wasn't his. But, I wanted them to know the truth. That's why my son has my last name. He would not tell his family.

"When I come home, since I have some money stashed away, I'm not going back to that life. We're gonna be straight," he said.

I was like, "Okay. Well, how long do you have to be in there?"

He said, "They told me 90 days, but my PO told me I may can get out in 45 if I found me a job. When I get out on my pass, they're going to let me go look for a job."

TD got a job at a car wash. He told this lady there that his girl was pregnant with his son and was getting ready to have his baby.

"She found out she was pregnant right after I went away."

So that's how he wound up getting out a little early, so to say. He found the job the first week they let him go out on the pass. TD already had a car before he went in, and it had been sitting. He went and got his car and would come and pick me up. I'd go to the car wash with him for a little bit, then I'd take the car and go whatever I needed to go. I was driving by then. I was getting ready to be 17 and he was getting ready to be 22. We were still inseparable and were together every day. Just like old times.

We created quite the family together despite everything against us. Glory be to God, in June of 1997, our baby was born. I was still 16. That following month, because my birthday is in July, I turned 17. A month after that, TD and I decided to take things further. We made the choice to find a place to move into together. That was in August, right before my senior year of school started.

CHAPTER 7
The Knight & The Princess

This was about a month after my 17th birthday. We wound up getting a place together and I found a better job. I was going to school and working a full-time job. TD was working too. He was back in the game and working at the car wash. Working my full-time sales job, I actually was making the kind of money of the average 30 year old. So, in my senior year, I dropped out of school.

The car wash TD was working at was owned by an older guy that we had met named Raulo. He was getting older and he wanted TD to learn the business so he could eventually start running it. Because Raulo's sell price was so cheap, TD was interested in trying to work with him to eventually buy the wash. Raulo kind of became like a godfather to TD and me, even though we were grown. He knew our stories. He knew about TD being in the game and he knew we had a child we were raising together.

"Look man, you got a kid and you have a good girl," Raulo told TD one day. "I don't want to see you get caught up again out here."

TD listened a little. He kind of worked at the car wash and still did his thing on the side. At the time, we had a two-bedroom apartment. It was just him, Baby G and me. Then, one day my great aunt (the one I had lived with when I was a kid and she had breast cancer) called and said she and her husband were taking a group of people to the amusement park we have here called Cedar Pointe.

"We got some extra tickets. You and TD should come. Get out and have some fun," she said.

"We want to go, but I don't know if we're gonna come," I told her.

"Well, let me know," she said. "We're going in about a week, so let me know if you guys are coming."

I talked to TD but, at that time, my mother was coming in town. She lived in Oklahoma and was coming to visit. She had never met my son, so this was her visit to meet Baby G for the first time.

Baby G was my mother's first grandchild. She was excited about seeing him. Our relationship was better than it had ever been. I mean, it was rocky, but it was there. When she came, she immediately started trying to help me. It felt good to feel care from my mother. I always knew she loved me and cared about me. It was just good to be cared for and nurtured by her.

"You've got so much on your plate and in your little life," she said. "Why don't you let me take the baby back to Oklahoma with me for the summer."

. "You really wanna take him back with you?"

She said, "I want to get a chance to bond with my grandson. Just let me take him for the summer and you guys can have the summer to yourselves."

TD and I agreed that my mother could take Baby G to Oklahoma with her when she leaves. She was beaming the day they left, and I had mixed feelings. There was a lot going through my mind. It was the following week TD and I wound up going to the amusement park with my great aunt and her husband. Like I told you, my great aunt didn't have children, so I was her like her child. Remember, she's the one who named me and everything. Time we left Cedar Pointe, TD and I went to our apartment and went to sleep because he had to get up and go to work the next day. I had to get up and go to work too.

Around two o'clock in the morning, I just started having this excruciating pain. I couldn't even walk. I rolled out the bed onto the floor. It felt like I was having really, really bad cramps I finally started screaming and calling TD's name.

He awoke startled and frantic, "What's wrong?"

I was like, "I don't know. All I know is this is the worst pain ever."

We were thinking maybe it was my appendix because of how I was hurting so bad on my side. As TD prepared to get me to the emergency room, I told him to give me a minute so I could get myself together. Baby G had been gone with my mom for only about. I was sitting in the bathroom on the toilet crying, "Oh my, God," as the pain hit and the and next thing I knew, a big blood clot just fell out of me. I stood up and blood started running down my legs then I started having cramps and another clot fell out of me. I turned on the water and got in the bathtub because I knew I had to hurry up and get clean so TD gets me to the emergency room.

Then, TD walked in. He tried to keep it together as much as possible. He was trying to clean me up as I told him what happened. I asked him to grab me some pads for the ride to the hospital since I didn't know what was going on. Thankfully, he had the wherewithal to scoop up the blood clots that fell out of me in the toilet and on the floor. When we got to the hospital, we found out I was pregnant and was having a miscarriage. I didn't know I was pregnant. I went to that amusement park, got on all those roller coasters, got thrown around and stuff.

From miscarrying the baby, I couldn't get everything out. They had to give me surgery. I had to have a DNC to get everything cleaned out right. That was traumatic for me. Not that I wanted another baby, but the fact that that was another their loss in my life. You know, that was another loss for me. On top of that, TD didn't have any children, but he has stepped up to be Baby G's dad. It really cut us deep.

So, fast forward. I turned 18 and I called my momma and asked her to bring Baby G back home. I was missing my baby terribly. I was talking to him and stuff like that, but I wanted my baby back. He was walking and now running. They had him playing football and he was the mascot for my brother's football team. I felt like I was missing out because Baby G was the only somebody outside of TD that I felt like it was like "it's me and you against the world".

So, after miscarrying and feeling like I was missing out on so much of Baby G's life, I was ready to get out of Ohio at that moment. I wanted to start over, and I wanted TD to see other ways of living. Even though they lived in Ohio, his family had a very limited scope of the world and their opportunities.

TD's mom was from the backwoods of Alabama. She was a sweetheart. She moved to Ohio when TD was two. The man she met who eventually became TD's stepdad was a kingpin. He's actually the person who introduced TD and all of his brothers to the game. That's how TD got into the dope game in the first place. Slanging was the family business basically. And since Laura liked to gamble, we used to play Pity Pat all the time at the gambling houses. Laura had moved in with us for just a little bit while her apartment was getting ready. I kept telling TD that I had an uneasy feeling about Ohio and wanted us to get out of Akron.

"There's nothing here for us," I told him. "My mom already has the baby. So, we should go to Oklahoma and try something different."

TD had never been anywhere other than Alabama and Ohio. I'd lived a few different places and had been to several states when I was younger. And even though I was missing my baby, I wanted TD to get out of the game just as much. I knew the only way to get him out was to get him away from it. As long as he was still in Akron, he wasn't going to stop doing what he was doing because he was addicted to lifestyle. Even though he wasn't your typical drug dealer, that world was all he knew.

TD was a good man. He wasn't disrespectful. He wasn't a cheater. He was really quiet. He was real laid back. But, if he talked, you better listen. Unlike most dealers, TD wasn't flashy. He was not your typical plug. He fit none of the check marks. So, I kept telling him I thought we should relocate to Oklahoma for a fresh start.

"The baby is already there with my mom. We should just go to Oklahoma, start over, and try to build a life out there outside of Ohio," I urged.

At that time, all of TD's friends were going to jail and all kinds of stuff was happening. I told him I wanted a better life for us. It took a little bit of convincing. I can't explain it, but Akron seems to get a hold on people. It's hard to get people away from there. I never stopped mentioning Oklahoma and moving. TD finally agreed to relocate.

I was so happy, I immediately started preparing. I did a yard sale. We did a "Going Away" sale. And we had people that we knew too coming to our apartment and buying stuff the other sales didn't move. We, basically, sold everything except for our clothes. We put whatever we could fit in the car, and the rest we shipped to my mom's. Then, we got on the road and drove to Oklahoma. This was mid-1998.

We would stay with my mom for just a short time.. So, we packed up, got on the road, drove to Oklahoma, got there, and TD was definitely a fish out of water. He was still on probation from when he had gotten out of jail. But, thankfully, his PO was nice enough to let him report in by mail.

TD had a paper he had to fill out every month saying he didn't have any contact with the police. He'd have to state that he didn't do this, and he didn't do that. So, when we got to Oklahoma, we both immediately started job hunting. Then, I started going around looking for public housing too. The transition was kind of hard for TD because he didn't have any employment history except for Raulo's car wash. As Thanksgiving rolled around, TD was homesick because he'd never been away from his family like this before. He was a momma's boy who loved his mother immensely. I loved her too.

I understood how hard it was for him to be away from his mother and siblings for the first time in his life (except for when he went to jail that time). I could see he was struggling with his thoughts about staying in Oklahoma or going back to Ohio almost every day. Sometimes, he'd talk to me about how he was feeling.

"I keep having this back and forth. Do I want to stay? Do I want to go back?" TD admitted.

I kept saying to him, "What are we going back to? Let's get our life together. Your momma said she was open to coming here, but we just gotta get our stuff together so that we can get our place and do that."

Well, my grandmother, my great-grandmother and some of my family members came down from Ohio for Thanksgiving. For about a week before they came, I was just so sick. I kept feeling like I had the flu. I kept feeling nauseated. I went to the hospital and they told me that I was dehydrated and that I had a urinary tract infection. They put me on medication for the UTI and I just kept feeling like I was really sick.

Also, my period was supposed to come the week before and did not show up. I told TD that and admitted that I was thinking I might be pregnant. I told him I wasn't sure since the doctors said the UTI medication could throw off my cycle and was going to make me nauseated. When my family were all gathered and the house was abuzz, I sneaked out to my car. I drove straight to the store and bought a home pregnancy test. When I got back, I slipped in and told TD.

My mind raced. *Oh my gosh. If I am, I can't tell my mother. What am I gonna do with this baby?* I rushed to the bathroom and peed on the stick, with TD waiting in there with the shower running to throw off anyone who saw us both go in. We both sat there waiting patiently. Those minutes felt like hours.

"My God," I said as I saw the first line appeared. "It says one line means you're not pregnant and two lines mean you are."

That's when the second line came down. I got off the toilet and said, "We're pregnant again, but how am I going to tell my momma? What am I going to say?"

I was nervous. TD wasn't concerned about my mom's or anyone else's reaction. He was happy and excited. It hurt when we lost our child a few months prior. This time, though, we knew about the pregnancy early and were ready to take precautions because this would be TD's first borne child. We decided to devise a plan to tell my mother the news together but away from everyone else. We wanted her to be the first to know, but not find out in front of other people in case her reaction was going to be crazy. We wanted to be sure we didn't put her in any position to feel put on the spot and that I didn't feel put on the spot. So, on Thanksgiving Day, the family was in there cooking and I caught my mom's attention.

"Ma, come back here to our room. I got to tell you something," I beckoned.

When she came back there, TD was sitting on the bed and I was standing by the bed.

"TD and I got something to tell you," I said.

She looked at me and she looked at him.

She looked at me again and said, "I already know."

Then, she looked at him and said, "She's pregnant."

TD and I looked at each other. We were puzzled. We were wondering how she knew. I had gotten the package and box out of the bathroom trash, put it in a bag, put that bag inside a bag, and then threw the bag in the big trash can so no one would ever find out. We asked her how she knew.

"When she was doing all that throwing up and stuff, I already knew what it was. I knew it wasn't from no antibiotics or none of that. She's glowing," my mom said.

We were kind of surprised by her positive reaction. After that, I was looking at him like, *This kind of just went over well.*

After the Thanksgiving holiday, I went for my first checkup. I had been pregnant a little while because that was in the end of November. My baby was due in July. So, I was already like two months pregnant. I had to be pregnant when we went to Oklahoma or got pregnant right when we got there. It was during my first checkup that the medical staff found some concerns. They told me that, when they drew my blood, some of the counts that they look for in babies to check the baby to make sure they were not going to have Down Syndrome were off. To make sure they were getting accurate readings, I had to do all of these tests. A number of them still came back abnormal. They thought my daughter was going to be a Down Syndrome baby.

At four or five months, I had to get what they call an amniocentesis – where they stick this big needle in your stomach and draw the fluid from around your baby. So, they did that, it was at four months pregnant, and they told me that they would let me know if she was going to have Down Syndrome. TD was really ready to go back home now. He felt like, with his mom and family there, they could help us with the baby.

"I need to be able to make more money because now I got more responsibilities," TD said. "I'm getting ready to have a bigger family and I'm not finding employment like I want to here. They want me to work for pennies! I can't support my family off that."

TD promised me that, if we moved back to Akron around his family, he was not going to get back in the game. So, after preparation, we called his mom. He told her everything that was happening with him and what was going on with me. He told me that, when we moved back, we would have to stay with her in her apartment until we found an apartment of our own.

She was like, "Okay. Y'all can come whenever."

I was still waiting on the test results to come back. They told me it would take a few weeks. I was still waiting to find out if our baby was going to have Down Syndrome or not. In the meantime, informed my mom of the move so she could get in her last bit of time with Baby G. Then, TD and I packed our stuff up to go back to Ohio to stay with his mom.

Who was not a team player and happy camper? Who was livid? It was my momma. She did not want me to go back to Ohio. She did not want me to take Baby G with me if I still decided to go. She was attached to him. She did not want me to take my baby back. You already know, she was mad at me when I did. She acted like I had, I don't know, stolen something from her. She was angry. She wouldn't talked to me for a while. She was heated

We packed up, got Baby G, and moved back to Ohio to stay with TD's mom. But, we weren't there long. I went and applied for an apartment time we got there and handled some other business. I went and filled out the applications for public housing, food stamps and other assistance for my family as well. And, of course since I was pregnant, they were gonna move me to the front of the list.

So, while we were at his mom's house that month and a half, I got a phone call saying that they had an opening in some projects not too far away and that I could come look at them. At that time, that particular one (Summit Lake Apartments) was about the most decent housing project in the city. So, I went to go look at a unit in Summit Lake, did my interview, and they ran my background check.

Since I hadn't been in trouble, all I had to do to get the place was pay a little deposit. I paid the deposit and got the keys. We started, slowly but surely, getting furniture and stuff for the baby because she was getting ready to come. But, TD was not keeping his word at all. He was already back in the game.

When I found out, it was like, *What can I do?* We were back, we weren't moving anywhere, and knew we were going to be in Akron at Summit Lake until we found a house. TD was off probation at that time. They had let him off while we were in Oklahoma and completed it. My guess is that it was shortly after we arrived in Ohio that TD got back in the game.

Months after we move, we celebrate Baby G's birthday and July rolls around. The hospital said they were gonna schedule me for a C-section. The OB-GYN came in and explained to me exactly why. In general, she said, I was just different, and all my children will have to be delivered via C-section for the rest of my child-bearing years. Considering what all I went through while having my son – all those days of labor pains with virtually no dilation only to end up getting a C-section, I had no problem accepting the diagnosis.

My obstetrics gynecologist explained that I was just not opening up during Baby G's delivery. She said what was happening was my cervix wasn't dilating although I was in full-blown labor with my son. Over the course of the two days, the most I dilated was two centimeters. I can't remember the medical terminology for it right now. But, when I grew up, my pelvis never matured.

Because of this pelvis abnormality, I can't deliver babies naturally. When most other women have babies, their pelvises open up for the babies to pass through the wombs and their cervixes dilate several centimeters. My body doesn't do that because I still have the pelvis of a little girl, they said. They figured that out after I went through what I did with my son. When my daughter came, we already knew I needed to have a C-section because it had been well-established that, unless it was a miscarriage or stillborn, I could not deliver a baby vaginally at full term. They scheduled me for the section.

On July the 10th, 1999, little Tatiana made her way into the world. She was healthy, beautiful and already had personality. Right after I had her though, I got a phone call from my mother about my brother. That call came after my birthday though. I had Tatiana on the 10th and, 11 days later, I celebrated my 19th birthday.

TD and I were getting ready to be married. My great-grandmother, after I had my daughter, told us that was the right thing to do. She was real old school. She was my maternal grandmother's mother – my mother's mom's mother. They called her Queen.

She said, "If you gone be making a family with her, she's good enough to have baby, she gotta be good enough to be your wife."

So, she basically made us marry. We didn't have no traditional wedding, big wedding or anything like that. We had a private ceremony at the church. It was us, our kids, my brother, a couple people that we knew, and our pastor. This was in August of 1999.

After we got married, we went up to Michigan with my dad for what we call our little honeymoon. We went to this place up there that he'd told us about. We left the kids with TD's mother, my mother-in-law.

Prior to that, it had been over a year since I had seen my dad. When I moved back from Oklahoma, my dad was already living in Michigan after he had gotten out of jail. As you know, he had been in and out of jail and on and off drugs my whole life. He went from selling drugs to doing drugs, but he was clean now. He wanted to get away from Ohio but be somewhere close enough where he could come home and visit family here. So, he moved to Michigan while I was in Oklahoma. I can't think of the name of the city my dad moved to, but it is a little suburb right outside of Detroit.

When the honeymoon weekend at the resort was over, TD and I went back home. It was life as normal after we get back. A month later, in September, I get a phone call from my mom. I hadn't been talking to her on a regular. I told you, when we left, she was pissed at me. She did call me when I had my baby girl and she did wish me a happy birthday, but it wasn't the same.

This call, two months after my birthday, wasn't like a regular conversation that we had either. She was saying my middle brother, Mitch, got in some major trouble at his school and she couldn't deal with him anymore. He was giving her the blues. They had expelled him from school, she said. I think they had said it was for terrorism or some stuff because he threatened somebody.

"I can't do it no more! He's kicked out of school. He can't go back, and he needs to be in school somewhere," Ma said.

So, she sent my 15-year-old brother to come live with me and my family. I was 19, and she sent my 15-year-old brother that she couldn't handle to me. We got him in school, and it was like I had another child. My middle brother already looked at me like I was his momma because I was the mother figure in my brothers' lives since our mother was always working to provide for us.

Mitch always told people, "This my sister mom."

I had gotten him on the right track for a minute. And then, next thing I know, he was in the game too. TD had put him on. At this point, I'm like, I want to go back to school. I dropped out of school my senior year because what I had responsibilities. I wanted to go back to school because I knew that I wanted to do something with my life and drugs and all of that stuff was not what I wanted to do. So, I put my kids in daycare and went back to school at night while I was working during the day.

My brother was in school and my husband was working. Both were also still in the game on the side. I decided I'd stop nagging them about their choices. My focal point became me and my kids. As for anyone else, I felt like they could do whatever they gotta do for themselves. My mindset was changing because now there were kids involved. I had to do something with my life. *I've gotta have something to give my babies because I know what it feels like for nobody to have nothing to give me.*

When I dropped out, I was only a few credits from graduating. So, I went to night school for only like six months and was finished. I was so proud of myself when I graduated in December 1999. It felt good to walk that stage. My dad came. My kids were there. My brother was there. You would've thought I would have had a bigger support system, but I didn't. So those people were the only ones I had there. My mom didn't live here and wasn't able to come. But my dad came, and he brought the lady he was dating at the time. Her name was Kay. After graduation, I began to think about college. *I think I want to go to college. I want to go to school. I want to do something with myself.*

I kept telling TD, "I want to own me a business one day, so I want to go to school."

I went and signed up to start college for the following year for business. I went to the University of Akron, took my admissions test, and was accepted. In January of 2000, I got accepted into college and I started school.

CHAPTER 8
The Grass Looked Greener

TD was still doing his thing. My brother was driving me crazy. He was in and out of trouble, but not as bad as he was when he was with my mom. That was hard. You know that, if you ain't gonna listen to your mama, you definitely ain't gonna listen to me. At the end of the day, I wasn't even 20 years old and I was trying to teach a teenage boy how to be a man and he was just three years from being grown himself. So, once I started college, I knew I had to have a talk with Mitch and TD about life directions eventually.

TD was real laid back. He was a quiet person who never messed with nobody. This one day, I got home a little later than usual one day from class. When I pulled up, I saw TD arguing with the boyfriend of the lady who lived the next building over. I got out of the car puzzled.

"What is going on?"

I was told the guy was speeding through the parking lot and TD told him to slow down, then things escalated. I guess our neighbor's boyfriend, who was known for popping pills and stuff, was high or something. They said he almost hit the kids playing outside. And since TD was outside watching our kids play, he naturally said something to the guy.

"You almost ran my kids over! Why is you doing that stupid stuff? Why are you even driving through the parking lot like that?" TD lectured.

Since I'd gotten out of the car, I started talking to the girl whose boyfriend he was. Me and her were cool. Our families knew each other. But, you know how people are when they're on drugs – very erratic. While me and her were talking, the guy started acting crazy, talking crazy to TD, and her baby's daddy hauled off and punched TD. What did he do that for? A brawl ensued.

A whole fight breaks out. The guy's family was in their apartment and our family was outside – some of my family and a couple of TD's relatives. Of course, my family done stomped these dudes out time they got involved because that's what my family was known for there. Me and the girl whose Kids father it was were standing there looking like we were in a state of shock because we couldn't believe this was really happening.

What started as an argument between two people had now grown into a group of people fighting like cats and dogs. Finally, the fight got broken up. One of the neighbors called the police. The police came and told everyone that didn't live in apartments to leave and for those who lived there to go inside. Once we got upstairs, we talked about everything that had just happed. I felt like I was only getting bits and pieces of the story.

"What is going on? What happened?" I couldn't help but ask.

As we were sitting around talking, we decided to order us some food. TD started telling me what happened from the beginning to the end. Some people pulled up in the middle and didn't know what was going on but still joined in the fight just because they saw their family members fighting. They didn't even know what they were fighting for.

Maybe a couple of hours later, we were laughing off how stupid the whole situation was. The next thing we knew, we heard popping. Then, bullets came flying in and we realized they were shooting up my apartment. I grabbed my kids, go upstairs, and put them on the floor. *This can't be real life. This can't be real.*

Thank God my daughter wasn't sitting in her highchair because one of the bullets came through the wall and lodged in the back of her highchair. Since my family was still there, some of them came out of my house shooting back. Others were shooting back from inside my apartment. When the police finally came, they said they counted over a hundred and something shell cases outside.

The next day, I went to class. When I got home, I had a three-day notice on the door to evacuate the premises because our projects were property of the state. So Now we had to find somewhere we can afford to move to with our kids. Even though the notice said we had to leave in three days, they wound up giving us about 21 days.

Well, we got up out of there by the end of the month. We had found a house to rent for $600 a month. We paid the security deposit, finished packing, and we kept working. Then, we paid the first month's rent and, the following month, moved into the house. While we were there, though, TD ended up getting into trouble.

"Okay. I've got to pay full rent now that you're in trouble and going back and forth to court," I acknowledged.

When he went to jail, he didn't go for an extended period of time. They actually sent him to jail twice. The first time was for three months. Then, he came home. He went to jail again for four months. That last time he came home, he was different. I had to let him know.

"I can't really . . . I don't want this life," I told him. "We gotta do better."

The summer was over. We were into the Fall of 2000 when he came out. I was 20 with two babies. I wanted him to change. Our children needed him to change. After that second time he went and came home, I gave him an ultimatum.

"I can't keep doing jail with you," I told him. "Look, you either want this life or you want your family. You choose. Because, what I'm not going to do is allow my children to be taken away from me because the police kicked the door in because you're selling drugs or somebody come in here trying to rob us, kill us, and kidnap us because you're selling drugs. You've made enough money in this life that we can take it and do something legitimate with it."

But what I realized, dear friend, was that it wasn't about the money. TD was addicted to that life. When he came home, he was

67

different. He kinda had disconnected from life. He disconnected from me. We didn't do stuff anymore. We didn't have fun together like we used to. We didn't do anything. I felt like we had, at that point, nothing more than an arrangement because it was just like everything was about the kids. It was nothing about him and me.

The simple fact that I hated his lifestyle kept a wedge between us. I was in a depression and didn't realize it. I was a functional, depressed person. I would go to work every day. I would still show up to classes. But, in the mornings, I didn't want to get out of bed. I didn't want to do much of anything. It was like my life had done a 180. *Who is this person? I don't even know who he is. This not the person that I remember.* It was like, every time he went to jail, it took a piece out of him. *I really don't want to do this.* But in his mind, he felt like he didn't have a choice. I felt like I was losing the one person that was down for me through everything. And, all because I gave him an ultimatum.

Monday through Friday, at that time, I would leave work and go to school and then come home. That was my life. Eventually, I started going out to bars. I didn't go out to bars and stuff and that. That wasn't even my style. I started going places with TD's cousin, Denise. She knew what was going on. I even started drinking. I really didn't like alcohol because it burned my stomach. But, I drank it anyway.

So, one weekend, I tell TD I was going out and I actually went out with his cousin Denise to a bar. I just was telling her what was going on with me and TD as we were sitting there talking. I shared with her some of what we had been dealing with and what we were going through. I was very honest with her about how our relationship was falling apart.

"I just feel like it is an arrangement. I don't feel like we are in love no more. And, I don't want that life for my children," I told Denise.

And while I'm sitting there talking to her, this guy walked up to us out of nowhere.

"Let me buy y'all a drink," the stranger said.

I didn't think nothing of it. Like I said, we were just sitting there drinking and talking. She was going through some things in her life and I was going through some things in my life. Denise and I had a relationship and we confided in each other.

I wanted things to work with me and TD. But, he was listening to the wrong people. They didn't want him out. He was the person that all of them went to. I was telling him to get out. They were trying to keep him in. It was a struggle.

"Oh, she thinks she's better than us. She thinks she all this cause she go to school," they used to say.

The truth was none of that was the case. Every chance I got, I helped them. My mother was so mad at the way I was being talked about and mistreated by some of TD's people. My mother was heated. She was real upset about that.

"You're barely grown yourself and that they all way older than you," she fussed.

You see, TD's siblings were older than him. TD was the baby. And, remember, he was five years older than me. Even though they were all way older than him, we were the ones helping them. Anyway, with all this continuing on, I kept going out every weekend. That was my release. TD was either gambling or doing his thing. This was my way dealing with things.

Denise and I would usually go to the same hole in the wall. We really liked their wings. It wasn't a big nightclub that would be packed with people on the weekends. It still drew a good crowd though because of the food and drinks. I always enjoyed myself there.

One particular weekend, the same guy that bought us the drink a few weeks prior was there. He was there with a female. Still, he got up and came over to where we were. *He just came in here with a female, so why is he over here talking to us?*

I think, at that moment, that I wanted out of my marriage. I was over it and I knew the bad parts were not going to change. I knew TD wasn't gonna change. Denise went to the restroom and I stayed there with the gentleman. I willingly entertained this new man. Eventually, I started talking to Zee. I did it.

I liked his hair cut. I liked the way he had the hair on his face trimmed. I liked the way he smelled. I liked the way he talked. I liked the way he dressed. And I liked the way he treated me and the people I loved.

Initially, like I said, I was "talking to" Zee. Just talking. The same way I did with TD in the beginning. We were just talking on the phone. Then, probably about three or four months in, we went out on a date. Being with him was so easy. He was outgoing, ambitious and overall cool. That first dinner was nice. He even gave me flowers.

"I know y'all situation, you know, but I'm just bringing you flowers and I'm taking you to dinner. I'm not trying to do nothing sexual with you. I'm giving you what you're not getting," Zee clarified.

At that point, I was like, "Nah. I'm struggling with the fact that I'm even having dinner or going out to eat with somebody or accepting gifts from you. Now, you're making me feel like this is what I'm supposed to be getting and I'm not getting it."

Zee was way older than me and TD. He was in his 30s. Mind you, TD had a lot going on and had brought his game to the car wash. On top of that, he was making bold moves. For instance, they got a contract cleaning these police cars through the Sheriff's Department. While they would have police cars there, TD would still handle his business.

So, one day, I went up to the car wash where TD worked and had an epiphany. I had already been up there earlier to see what TD had going on, and he said he was just washing cars and doing the car wash stuff they be doing, I told him I was about to do some running around and asked him if he needed me to do anything for him.

He was like, "Not right now. But, later, can you drop me off something to eat?"

I told him I would. I didn't go right away, since he had said not to do it now. I waited about an hour and then I pulled up. When I parked, I saw one of the people that TD was serving pull up. Police and sheriff's cars were still there getting washed. I sat and watched TD complete the whole transaction. Something inside of me said, *It's time for you to get out of this.* I immediately called Zee.

I said, "What you doing?"

He said, "I'm getting dressed. What you doing? What you want to do?"

I was like, "I just need somebody to talk to."

He told me, "Pull up over here."

So, I rolled up on him. After I pulled up, I couldn't help talking about what I was dealing with, what I just saw, and how I didn't want to be in that life.

"I want better for me and my kids," I said.

That was when I couldn't help but notice how Zee had a good life. *I don't even know what this person does for a living.* I never heard talk about going to work, but I did see he had nice things. I wanted to ask about his income source, but I never asked. *I don't even wanna know about nothing.*

"I don't want to go from one person to doing the same thing with another person," I admitted. "I'm trying to do something with my life."

Zee said, "I know what you mean. I don't blame you for not wanting to go back to that life. I was in that life and I wouldn't go back to it either. I went to jail for that, so I'm good."

I was content hearing that. His admission eased the uncertainty I was feeling about him. Slowly but surely. Zee started to introduce me more and more to his life. I eventually learned how he was making his money. He and his circle were into the check game.

The check game they ran was full scale. They were getting routing and account numbers from corporate offices to make sure they were using business accounts. Then, they made checks themselves payable to whatever name they wanted. They were also having people get bank accounts and deposit those checks. When the checks would go through at the store for a big-ticket item, they'd go back and get cash in seven days. Sometimes, they'd make deposits through the ATM with the checks, or go in the bank and deposit the check so money would be available in three days.

Really, the money wasn't there. When the banks found out 10-21 days later, Zee and his crew already had the money and whatever merchandise they decided to keep. That was definitely something different for me. *Now, we done went from street crimes to white-collar crimes.* I had never seen anyone making thousands and thousands so fast like that. When I say thousands and thousands, I mean thousands and thousands and thousands and thousands of dollars. It got to the point where it was nothing Zee couldn't afford.

"I'm getting ready to take you on a trip," he said.

We were just hanging out, just doing stuff, just chilling. And I looked up and saw that it was three o'clock in the morning. I had never done that. I had never done anything like that before. I had never stayed out past one with Denise, even though the bars didn't close until two. Denise would usually drop me off at home and keep going. I knew TD knew our pattern and schedule.

Now that I was hanging out with this new person by myself and TD's cousin was no longer around, the evidence was beginning to show. Although I sneaked in the first night undetected, I was still nervous about coming in so late. That didn't really stop anything. It started happening more frequently. One day, I caught myself sneaking in at four o'clock in the morning.

I sneaked in through the back door. All the lights in my house were off. Ii came in through the back because the kitchen was in the back. My plan was to sneak in and get in the bed. I had done it several times. As soon as I got in the living room, the light came on.

"Where have been this time of night?" TD grunted.

We started arguing. I kept telling him the same thing over and over.

"I asked you to make a decision. I told you, you needed to make a decision," I reminded him. "Do you want your family, or do you want your lifestyle? Clearly, you picked the lifestyle."

He was like, "So you out messing with dudes? You're doing this?"

At that time, I hadn't done nothing with Zee, other than talk and spend time. We didn't have nothing sexual going on. We hadn't done anything. I tried to tell TD that.

"I'm not messing with nobody! You know I'm not sleeping with nobody," I told him.

Now that the cat was out of the bag, and TD knew everything, I didn't have to feel the guilt that I felt when I would come in late from hanging out late with Zee. So, I kept doing it. This went on for probably three or four more months. Then, one day I came home and told TD I was moving out.

"What did you say?"

"I'm getting the kids and moving out."

I told TD he could have everything in the house and that I was leaving him. I let him keep all the furniture and electronics. The only things I took with me and my kids were our clothes and my computer. I had saved a lot of money to buy my computer. It was my investment into my future. This move was my investment in my children's futures. My kids were four and two. I was 21 and Zee was 34. His kids were only a few years younger than me. Once again, I was looking for that father figure.

CHAPTER 9
Problems Seldom Cease

When we moved in with Zee, all hell broke loose. TD flipped the hell out. He had a breakdown and started acting crazy. I'd never seen him act like that before. I didn't understand why he was being so extreme. He was very far outside his character. You know how TD was. He was quiet and laid back. The next thing I heard, and he was dating a girl that was still in high school.

All I could say was, "What the hell?"

Here's the kicker. When I moved out with the kids to Zee's place, we moved just down the street from TD. That meant, we would see each other in passing. I had been seeing this teenage girl, Tasha, going over there. But, I didn't think anything of it until one day I saw her over there during school hours. She left before school was supposed to be out. I kept going back and forth in my feelings about this situation

For a minute, I was happy I got out of that life with TD and I felt relieved. But now, in the back of my mind, I kept second guessing myself and asking if I am making the right decision by being with Zee instead. TD would call me sometimes and want to talk. Life was like an emotional roller coaster. Five months went by.

One day, I saw that same girl leaving TD's house and she looked like she was pregnant. I was crushed. I didn't say anything.

Then, I heard that she was from the family and through the grapevine because everybody was talking about it. I was hurt all over again.

"You know TD got a baby on the way with that teenage girl?"

Even though I moved on, I caught myself using this new situation to try to make him change. After all, I was a teenager when TD started dating me. I knew that he was taking chances dating females so much younger than him. And, considering the risks he was already taking every day in the game, I didn't want to see him go to jail again – or even prison for that matter.

That was why I was distraught. I had to catch myself. I wanted to go over there, knock on the door, and say she had to leave and couldn't come back. My name was still on the house he was living in. That was another reason why I needed to have that talk with him. So, I went over there. Luckily for her, she wasn't there. He was though, and so we talked.

"You having a baby with a teenage girl? You could go to jail, bro," I told TD. "I'm know what I'm hearing cannot be true."

He was like, "Yup. Basically. You left me. You hurt me. Now, I'm about to hurt you and prove a point to you."

I figured he was trying to say he got that girl pregnant because I moved down the street from him. I just said okay and left it at that. So, one night I'm at Zee's house and I'm in the bed knocked out. I get up to go to the bathroom in the middle of the night and I notice there's no car outside. *What? My car is gone!*

I started blowing Zee's phone up. The phone was going straight to voicemail. So, I woke up Zee's kids, asking them if they knew where Zee could be. Trying to see if something was going on and that was why Zee was gone in my car. Zee's kids said there was no emergency going on that they knew anything about. I started calling hospitals at that point because I was worried that something may have happened. That was when the kids let me in on a little secret. Zee had a drug problem.

I didn't know that. That was very weird to fathom because, like I said, Zee wore nice clothes, was always on point, and always grinded like me. So, I never knew. I would have never known had I not gotten up and saw my car was gone. At this point, I wondered, *What the hell did I get myself into?* Zee was a functional drug addict. And, here I was with feelings for a person who is a deceiver and master manipulator.

After I got past my anger, my nurturing side kicked in. I then began wondering, *How can I help get him past this?* I didn't want to become a crutch, but I did want to help Zee get his life back together without the drugs. I saw so much great potential when I watched him interact with the kids. When I got my car back the next day, I was an emotional wreck though. I was crying and asking question after question.

I'm like, "Why would you do this? Why wouldn't you tell me?"

Zee said, "That's just something that you don't go around broadcasting and telling people."

I said, "Well, I think that's something you should tell somebody with kids that's living with you.".

"You shouldn't do people like this. You should be upfront and let them choose if they want to deal with all this or not," I couldn't help but tell Zee. "You didn't give me an opportunity to choose. I can't trust you."

That was the truth the rest of the time we were together. I wouldn't even leave my money laying around. I had been in a relationship with this person for about 18 months. Now, the relationship started to get physical and unhealthy. We're in full dysfunction. We're in love one minute and physically fighting the next minute. We're arguing one minute and the next minute we are laughing. We're fully supporting each other one minute, and the next minute we want to sabotage what the other person is trying to do.

For the most part, I was isolated from my family. I talked to my mom periodically. Like I said, she didn't live in Ohio. But, she was trying to get me out of that situation long distance. Of course, she knew about what was going on with me because my family was blowing her phone up. My mom was trying to get me out of the situation and trying to see why I went and got involved with Zee in the first place.

"What got you in the situation? What happened to TD?" She asked.

I just told her everything. I had never expressed anything to anybody the way I did with my mom during that conversation. After that though, I still stayed in that relationship with Zee for six years. We were together from about 2000 all the way up to 2006.

Shortly after everything came out though, we moved and no longer lived down the street from TD. We moved to the other side of town and we were working. But it was like I was in a crack house, you know. I would be crying and talking about how I didn't want to be involved with him anymore.

Zee started telling me how he got hooked. He said he was smoking weed with a friend one day and didn't know the blunt was laced with a primo. He smoked it and got hooked on hit. That how Zee went from selling to using and wound up in prison for it.

"After I got out, you know, I wanted to get myself together and be there for my kids," he said.

Basically, he just couldn't get the monkey off his back. That was when I said we couldn't handle this by ourselves. Zee's problem was stronger than love and prayer can break.

"Let's get you some help," I said.

At this point, we keep working our gigs and holding things together while we move around a little bit on the other side of town.

It was nice to not be around TD and the pregnant girl, or that whole environment. It was like a new environment. We had new people that were hanging around, and we had different situations we found ourselves in. This moment also brought about a request that had never been asked of me up into this point.

"Let me show you how to get into this game with the checks," Zee said.

Despite being on drugs, Zee was still not hurting for cash because he still did checks on the side with his crew and daughter.

"If something ever happens to me, you got the kids and y'all can come up like that," he said. "You and the kids will always be good."

If you know one thing about me, I don't mess up money. I'm a good steward over money. Zee knew that too.

"You don't mess off money like me," he said. "I know you will be able to turn it into something or invest it."

I knew how to manage money well not because I grew up rich, as you know. I grew up early and had to provide for more than myself early. I'd always had a business mentality. I just didn't know which way to go with it. I also didn't know how to handle what Zee was wanting to teach me about his world. You know what I mean?

I was 23 at this point. I was still trying to go to school and work. I felt like life was just happening. I had my brother with me and my kids still. He transitioned from one relationship to another relationship with me. He was still in the game with TD too.

Since I had my brother and my kids, and Zee had his own kids, I decided to sit out of school the next semester. Instead of going to classes at the University of Akron, I was kind of just a student of Zee's crew. I spent time watching what they were doing and listening to what they were telling me and saying to each other. I didn't participate at first. I just watched and the analytical side of me started to critique what I saw.

We all know that, as time goes by, if you're doing the same thing and times are changing and technology is now changing but you're not changing, you're going to get swallowed up. One day I told them they have to be willing to change the things they were doing, or they were going to catch themselves up.

"You have to change what you are doing, the way you're doing it," I said. "Look, y'all probably should not be doing this. If you keep doing this, maybe you should do it like that. If you're going to do that, then maybe you should do it like this."

They were listening. It was a whole group of them. Even those way older than Zee were listening.

"Have you thought about this? What will happen if y'all get caught? Then what?" I asked them.

I didn't know anything about white-collar crime. I knew about drugs because many of the men in my life were involved with drugs. You know the story. My daddy sold drugs and used drugs. My uncle sold drugs and was still strung out on drugs. My brother sold drugs. TD, the man I regretfully still loved, sold drugs. I knew about drugs. But what Zee's crew was talking about with these checks, I didn't know nothing about the long-range of that.

I was like, "At some point, if something happens, what will go down? If y'all do get caught, will y'all go to jail? Will it be like y'all robbed the bank?"

When I first met Zee and thought Zee was a man rescuing me from the invisibility I felt with TD, I didn't want to know the details about the source of the lifestyle I saw. Now that everything was on the table, I wanted to be sure I wasn't in the dark again about anything going with Zee that involved me, directly or indirectly. Zee gave me plenty of reasons to not trust what he said. I had to be there and see things for myself and hear things for myself to know the whole of what was really going on if I were going to let Zee teach me what he wanted me to know.

I felt like I was so deep in with Zee, because me and my kids lived with him, that I had to try to make sure whatever he did worked out for the best. In the drug game, if something happened, I knew what to expect. The police would come kicking in your door, tear up everything in sight, take every adult to jail, and haul the kids off to state custody. I explained this to Zee 'nem.

"I don't know your game. I just know the games that I've been seeing or playing my whole life," I admitted. "What are the policies and procedures for your crew?"

One of the senior citizens in the circle said, "Oh, none. As long as the check is not over this certain amount, if it is a felony, it's only a fifth-degree felony."

A middle-aged member chimed in, "Even then, a lot of times, people just get probation. They don't need to get jail time because it's not like you had a gun. We go in the bank and we came out with a receipt. So, it's not like we're not properly transacting bank business."

I was like, "What? For real?"

My mind was blown. Mind you, I had an aunt who worked at the Akron Police Department still. You may recall my dad's sister. The one I told you was a police officer when I was a kid. She had been promoted to detective, or getting ready to be one, around this particular time. Anyway, I started asking her random questions after that session with Zee's crew.

She didn't why I would ask the questions that seemed out of the blue. She didn't even know about the kind of life I was living with Zee. So, I was asking what kind of questions to be sure I didn't get myself caught up in something because I wasn't getting the full story from Zee's crew. Who knows, maybe they were already told what to share and not share when I'm around. I asked my Aunt Renee some of the same questions I asked Zee's crew. I made it a point to squeeze in the main ones, even if it took more than one conversation and some creative play on words.

I would ask a question and she would tell me whether something was true or not. I would usually set it up as something I heard someone say and I just couldn't believe it was true. I wasn't lying. That really was the case, as you know. I was just careful to not say too much and trigger her detective nose.

"I heard some people was running checks and then we hear about people getting in trouble for checks. What I don't understand is are they going to jail for that for a long time because it seems to be a lot of people doing it," I said.

Aunt Renee was like, "Nah, it ain't no hard time. They be slapping these people on the wrists."

She didn't know I was asking questions because I was now caught up with a whole group of people that were doing that very thing. I knew she would tell me the truth and whatever she said would let me know whether what Zee and the crew were teaching me was on point. My aunt knew her stuff. She wasn't even a street cop no more. Yep, that's right. She was a detective at that point. I was shocked to find out the check game and white-collar crime was handled like that.

"It's one thing when you go in the bank with a gun. It's another thing when you're doing little stuff like checks," my aunt said.

I knew my dad had been in trouble for checks before, but I didn't know if he was doing the same thing Zee and his crew was doing or if he had been doing something totally different. I didn't know anything about the way my dad did any of his dirt. I just knew he found different things to do that kept his time with us limited.

My aunt was like, "Remember when y'all daddy was doing checks? He ended up having to do time though."

I was like, "Yeah, I remember. But, I didn't know what he was doing. I just knew he had got in trouble for checks."

She said, "Girl, they were dropping fake deposit slips in the ATM machine and then withdrawing the money out the next day. It wasn't even no real check in there. Your daddy would think of stuff like that."

We laughed. I was thinking how I knew a whole crew of people that were into that and some other things. Although I knew my mother and none of my family approved of my relationship with Zee but, I didn't let it affect my view of my relationship with Zee. That was something only Zee and I could end. I could tell my aunt had spoken to my mother recently. She shared some of the same sentiments. I wasn't going to have any of that from her either.

So, we just kept talking about things like we always did. She had no reason to believe things were not normal. But, in my mind, mind I was just like, *I don't know if it's just me being rebellious. I just don't want anyone to tell me what to do.* I was 21 and I loved Zee. You think you know it all at 21. You think nobody can tell you anything or can show you a definition of what you should be looking for in a mate.

You're just making decisions along the way and saying, "Well, this person did this for me, so they must love me."

That's the way it was for me, at least. I thought people must love me if they did things for me because that was the only way my father knew how to show love. He even did it with the women in his life. He never knew what the real definition of love was. He said it was because his mother was the same way.

My father was the same way. He would not apologize but would buy you something to try to compensate for it. I even found myself doing that with my kids until I realized that was a cycle that I didn't want to repeat. You know what I mean?

So, I kept studying the check game under Zee and his crew and was going on three years in my relationship with Zee. Every weekend, we were going out. This life wasn't even me. I felt convicted. I knew God. I just was not operating like I was taught. I would feel convicted and start questioning my behavior and my own thinking. *Why am I even here? Why am I at these clubs? I don't even fit in here.* It's not that I was uncomfortable. That just wasn't my lifestyle.

Unfortunately, my general habit was still defaulting to the mindset of "whatever they doing, that's what I'm doing" because I was still seeking acceptance and love. I had never been a follower, but I frequently made myself follow others because I wanted to be loved and accepted by them. That was the crazy part about it. I really wanted love and acceptance, and that was the whole reason why I wound up in the gang in the first place. Looking for love and acceptance was how I thought my then homeys loved me. That love and acceptance were what I was looking for when always choosing relationships with older people. I knew then that I was looking for someone who filled the void of that father figure, and I accepted that I was also trying to fill the void of that mother figure.

One day, my mother called. My baby brother was in college at this time, and me and Zee had moved our family a new house. We were living on the west side of town, which was where my where my mom lived. She had moved back to Ohio from Oklahoma. My baby brother was a football star. Wait. Let me slide all the way back. Follow me now.

She moved back Ohio after she left my stepdad! They moved back to Ohio because we had a major situation with my daughter, I had let my daughter go with her dad, TD, for the weekend and somebody did something to my daughter while she was over there. We don't know who did it to this day. They did a whole police investigation and everything. I called my mother because I was getting ready to go to jail. She came and, after talking to me and telling me what she was not going to stand for, she said she was moving back home.

That's what she did. She moved back to Ohio in 2003 because, she said, "I need to be there with you and my grandkids because I can't leave you there with those people. Somebody gotta see about my grandbabies. So, I'm moving back"

She really hated the relationships I had with TD and Zee. She especially was against my being with Zee, as you know. But, at this point, I was 23 years old and she couldn't do anything to make me leave Zee. Although our relationship was abusive, mentally and physically, I stayed because I loved knowing my kids were taken care of and they didn't have to want for a thing. Even though I knew my love for Zee was present yet waning, being in the relationship with him was about more than that. Making money with him was also about more than that because my kids were involved, and they made everything bigger than them.

All of that stuff was going to have to be cut out. We were unhealthy together. We'd fight and break tables. We'd do all kinds of stuff to each other when we were mad. It was nutts. We were nutts. So, she moved back. It worked perfectly since Matthew, my baby brother, was a football star. He played for Buchtel High School and all of these schools were looking at him. All of these colleges wanted him because, although he was only 16 or 17 at the time, he was a phenom. No one could stop him when he was coming.

We had NFL coaches come in and look at him, and they'd sit and watch him play ball. They called Matthew "The Train" because he could stop the whole football line by himself. He'd been that way since he was a kid in peewee football. He was a football star when we lived in Oklahoma. And then, when he came to Ohio with his style, they went wild. They hadn't seen anybody in the city do the things my baby brother did.

He was big and light on his feet. He had speed. He had strength. He had intellect, good sportsmanship, and a loveable personality. He had everything that they were looking for in a star football player. Soon after my mom moved back, we found her an apartment she liked, and we found her a good job.

At first, after she got back, she started getting real sick. She had been getting sick before, but now it was different. She was helping me with the kids any way she could, and she didn't have a good source of income since the job she had was only part-time. She was working as a home health aide. Her health problems didn't make some days any easier.

Matthew was living with our mom and excelling in school. Mitch was still living with me, and Zee our kids in our house. It became my job to support everybody with the little income I had coming in from my job working as a claims specialist at an insurance company. I knew I couldn't support everyone off that. I needed to be able to get more income and get it right away. That was how I got involved with what Zee and his crew were doing, even though I still did not know who was running the whole operation. I just got in where I could fall in.to get what I knew my family needed.

I was turning 24. I kept praying and asking God what I needed to do. I knew my mother needed me more than she ever had before. We both needed each other more than ever. My baby brother was getting ready to graduate and go off to college in a minute. We definitely didn't have money to send him to college, even with him going off some scholarship we were sure he'd get.

"Matthew is going to be the one that's gonna get us out of this situation," we all said.

Everyone who knew us knew that his thing was fulfilling his dream of going to the NFL. I could totally see him making it! Even though I was able to start making more money come through the door, I was still in the abusive relationship with Zee. Things didn't change much after Matthew left for college. The years of my turning 24 and turning 25 were basically the same and just flew by. Again, I was just going through the motions and existing, doing whatever I could do to make things happen for my family despite the abuse.

Periodically, during those years, Zee would show me how to do different stuff that I hadn't been shown before. The crew would tell me how to make it work out the best. Eventually, they showed me how to go into the stores and get stuff without the money. They taught me all about having the items charged to an account and not having to be on the account. But, the twist was, the companies could still find a check for the purchase. Remember, I was the youngest person in the group. A lot of them were old enough to be my grandparents, my parents. Nobody in the group my age.. I was the new kid on the block. The rest of them had been rolling together and doing things together for years. I only got introduced to it because of who I was rolling with.

I told them, "I'm not trying to be greedy. I'm just trying to get money to help my momma and my brothers and make sure I can pay my own bills. I'm not a lazy person. I'll go to work, but my work check is not getting me where I need to be."

In my mind, where I needed to be was in a position to better provide for my children and other family. All we had was each other to lean on. And then, with my mom being in and out of the hospital and my brother needing stuff for school, I knew I had to do something different because my check was not cutting it. I didn't want him getting off course and getting out here ruining his life. Mitch and I always saw eye to eye on protecting Matthew because we felt like he had a promising future.

I told my family, "If anybody is going to take the risk, I'll take the risk for everybody."

So, I go out there at 25 and do this check game. Next thing I know, after a few months into making moves with Zee and the crew, I got a card stuck on the door from the Financial Crimes Unit of the Akron Police Department. The card said for me to call them at that number. When I called them back, they started asking me about shit that was in my account that did not clear. They wanted to know where I got it from, how I got it, and this, that and the other.

I just told him, "A lady was selling a vehicle. I got it from her."

The good thing about it was that I had just bought a car from somebody. I told them I guess the lady I was buying a car from didn't know that the check she gave me would not clear. They told me this was my first warning. I should have taken heed.

"I you don't pay the money back for that check within the next the next 21 days, we are going to file charges against you for receiving stolen property," the Financial Crimes officer said.

Of course, that shook me. I had never been in any trouble, ever, with police. I had never been on the radar of the system like that. I didn't like this one bit. There was no comfort in it.

I was like, "Okay. I'm giving y'all that $700 back. I'm not going to jail for nobody. I'm not getting in trouble for nobody. Y'all can have y'all check and get y'all money back."

Within the next three days, I got the money from Zee to pay the bank back. They were actually a credit union. They just closed my accounts and said I could not have an account with them anymore. Even though that was my first warning on this check life, it was really my third warning that I had ever gotten about even being close to getting in some type of trouble with Zee. And, with them being a credit union, the whole situation was worse because they were a federal institution and play no games.

I kinda chilled out on that for a little bit. The money that I had got from it, like I said, I would not splurge with it but kind of like budgeted it instead. *If I'm giving my mom this amount for her rent this month and that amount for her bills or for their food, I still*

93

got this little bit that I can try to invest in something to try to make it grow. So, that's what I did, and I was still working.

When I got my taxes, I kind of just let that sit in my other bank account and just kind of pinched off of it so that I could make sure that my mother and brothers had what they needed, my kids had what they needed, and I had what I needed. Still with Zee, the abuse continued. And then, right before I turned 26, the infidelity started.

Now, other women are coming to me and threatening me. They are talking about they're messing with Zee and hit that. I was getting into it with women when we go places and at when I was at home. There was one woman in particular who made it a point to stand out. She was angry and was saying she was in a relationship with Zee. She saw us leaving a bar one night together at two o'clock in the morning and tried to run us off the road. They all knew Zee and I were together. Our town was small. Everyone had to have known we lived together. We had been living together and were in a relationship for five years at that point.

I called out to the Lord. In the midst of this all, I clung especially close to God. If nothing else, I did remember to still pray. I knew that, even though I knew I was doing things that were wrong, I wasn't being malicious and my honesty no matter what would be rewarded. God knew that many of the wrongs I committed were just to survive or for the best of someone else because of our desperate situations. I always just found myself being prayerful regardless of what I was doing in my life.

"Lord! Help me, Lord," I frequently petitioned.

I established my relationship with God a long time ago. One thing about my great-aunt who named me, since I've known her, she's always been saved. We have a joke in the family that we all still get a kick out of anytime we hear it. She always said she got saved when Mary was pregnant with Jesus. Our grandmother's sister instilled in all of us, from my mother on down, the need to have a personal relationship with God and to be thankful for the sacrifices of Jesus as we allow the Holy Spirit to move throughout our lives.

As you may recall, my great-aunt and her husband didn't have any children. So, they kinda raised my mother because grandmother had six kids and was a single mom and didn't have a husband. My mother's mother was working two and three jobs to support her six. I learned why my mother had tunnel vision when she was working her two to take care of her three when we were little. My mother's aunt instilled that relationship with God in all of us.

"Let me tell you, no matter what you do in life, you keep God first," she said.

Now that I was 25, my "no matter what" relationship with God was fully established. That's how I survived those years with Zee, I believe. Those first couple of years, I knew it was God that blessed me and protected the family I cared for with Zee. In year three, I would say, was when it became abusive. My fourth and fifth years were still abusive. And, of course, my sixth and final year with Zee had its fireworks. Through all those years, and even now that Zee long out of the picture, God had and has remained with me.

I know it was God who brought me though. I was the one kept in the dark and the last one to know the truth. Even TD knew, which was why he was going crazy. After I found out, I was the one who was under attack. People were assuming things about me that weren't true, and they were using the bad things I had gone through to validate their thoughts. People can be so cruel to others during their suffering sometimes.. Others said it was because my relationship with TD failed and I lost him to a younger woman. They even had me wondering if I really was the way they were saying I was. The only rumors they had circulating that had some truth to it was that sometimes I didn't want to have sex because I was raped.

Even with TD that came up, so I had no qualms with hearing that kind of talk though the grapevine because I knew there were times I would fight TD off me because I just hadn't dealt with that. But, there were so many other things people said about me that were very hurtful and flat-out untrue. Still, I had bigger fish to fry and was eventually able to shake all that off and move forward with Zee thanks to God's healing and mercy.

I had dealt with a lot. I am still dealing with a lot. Back then, Zee helped me any way possible; and, Lord knows, I felt obligated to Zee. My mother hated that. But, even that is God. All truths have to be told for you to see the truth about what I've lived.

Even you know, it would only be because of God moving that you would be able to do or survive the things I have and come out of the same situations I have. There has never been a worry-free period in my life where I could just do nothing and know that everything is okay and see everything work out for everyone I love. Still, I know I can try not to worry and that whatever work I am doing God will honor because all things do work out for the good.

There were people who wanted me to fail. There were people who wanted me and Zee apart so bad they were willing to kill us. There were loved ones of mine who hated how dysfunctional our relationship was, yet our attachment wouldn't weaken. For us, it wasn't about sex like other people made it out to be. Even you know it was not that at all. It was the fact that we chose to build together, and make sure each other and our loved ones and family were taken care of that kept us working out problems no matter how violently we may get physical or how mean our emotional or mental abuse would be as we hurled the darts at each other. Again, my mother hated everything about the situation and felt like, even with her bad health, my kids shouldn't be around the toxic environment Zee and I had going on for five years now.

My mother was born in 1963. Zee was born in 1967. Zee was only four years younger than my mom. Because of this, I had moments where I was angry because I felt like I had been manipulated, which I had been. I had to just accept responsibility and get over that. I was the one who chose to stay after I found out. I was also the one who agreed to learn about the check game from them. Zee opened up a whole new world to me. Once I got a feel for how fast and hot this check game can get, I made sure we paid the people their money back even though we still kind of stayed in that realm. That came in handy periodically. If something happened or money was tight, we knew he had options and didn't have to keep struggling. I always knew I could go back to this and do that.

That's why our kids would way, "We rich!"

When I say our kids got a lot of things for Christmas, they got truckloads of stuff at Christmas time. Zee and I went out and got whatever the kids wanted. Even the kids in the neighborhood thought we were rich. It was like we were Robin Hood. We looked out for everybody and made sure no families in our neighborhood went without. People always thanked us.

"They buying us stuff and helping us."

"You don't know how much this is helping me."

"This is right on time."

"Thank y'all!"

We were always helping the less fortunate. That's why, when we were running the games, I would never take from a person. I would only take from a store or a business establishment because I knew they had insurance on their stuff. I knew what it was like to be less fortunate. I didn't want to add to no hardship that some poor person was dealing with. I would never take anything from nobody. Basically, we were taking the stuff and giving it to people. We helped so many families. I'm telling you! We gave away far more than we even kept or returned for cash. I can't even count how much stuff Zee and I gave away to people in need.

CHAPTER 10
Period of Loss

Now, I'm still 25. You already know about my brothers, but I had a little sister too, through my father. We had different mothers, but we were really close all our lives. Sirena looked up to me. I couldn't do no wrong in her eyes. We were really, really close.

At that time, she was working at McDonald's and her mom started having problems. Shortly after that, we found out she was pregnant. This was 2005, I think. I had gotten a phone call saying my sister was pregnant. Now, she was 16 and pregnant. I had a conversation with her.

"What's your plan? What are you going to do, as far as the baby?" I asked.

Sirena said, "I'm gonna continue to go to school and I'm gonna still work my job. I'm gonna have my baby and I'm just going to be there for my baby."

So, I just started mentoring her.

"Look, I know what it's like. I had my baby at 16," I reminded her.

We were already close, because she looked up to me like her role model. She wanted to be my protege so bad. She would, periodically, come stay with me when she and her mom got into it or whatever. But that talk brought Sirena and I closer than ever.

"We can't be upset," I told her.

We were excited about the baby. Having worked at McDonald's, I knew McDonald's was not paying nowhere near what she needed. McDonald's wasn't offering giving no life-changing money. I decided I would help my sister with her baby as much as I could. The months flew by. In my mind, that's when I really started saying to myself, *Look, this cannot be the example since you're the oldest sibling.* I have two brothers with my momma, and I have a brother and a sister with my dad. I am the oldest out of all of them. I told myself, *I gotta be the one to set the example for them so I can't be the person that's not doing what I'm supposed to do.*

I kept telling God, "I gotta get myself out of this situation. I've got to get out of it! My sister is getting ready to have another baby."

The new year came in. I told Sirena everything was going to be get better for us.

"Girl, this year going to be our year. You're gonna have my nephew or my niece, and I'm going to make sure I'm there for you every step of the way," I said.

By this time, college recruiters and all kinds of people had started coming to my mom's house. I remember one recruiter who, at the time, used to be an NFL coach for the Miami Dolphins. He was going into the college realm to become a college football coach. He was recruiting heavily while talking to my mom.

"I want your boy to come play for my team up in PA. I build you a house, buy you a house, whatever you want from me," he said.

I was thinking, *Oh, Lord! You've answered our prayers. This is how everything is gonna be better.* I was always praying for better for my family. *My brother's gonna make it! This is how we're going to get out of this situation.*

Then came March 5th, 2006. Let me back up to the day before. Like I told you, we were just excited about the baby and excited about what Sirena told me that she wanted to do with her life. So, it was March 4th that she called me.

"What you're doing tomorrow?" She asked.

I said, "Well, I'm going to a card game. But after the card game, I'm going home to cook."

She was like, "What you cooking?"

I said, "I don't know if I'm gonna make some fish or I'm gonna make some chicken."

She said, "That's crazy. That's why I called you. I wanted you to make me some fish, and some potatoes and onions."

Sirena always was craving.

"So, are you going to come over and spend the night?" I asked.

"Yeah, I'm gonna come," she told me. "I'm gonna just come tomorrow when I get off work. But, I'm going to the funeral first."

The funeral she was talking about was the one for a guy a lot of us knew. He was a young man. But, he had been abusive to his daughter's mother. He had been beating on that girl for years. He jumped on her. She was scared.

You know those little pairing knives that people use to maybe slice fruit or something like that real fine? She had a little paring knife in her hand when he jumped her. She might have swung it at him to get him to back up off her. I just know the paring knife went straight into his heart and killed him.

When my sister said she was going, I asked her who she was going to ride to the funeral with. I told her I was not planning to go to the funeral, but I would send something to his family's house. Since I knew the girl's family and his family we were just neutral in the situation.

"I'm not going to the funeral. I'm going to go to the card game. But, I am going to send food to the family's house where they are having the repass at," I explained.

Sirena said, "Well, I gotta work tomorrow and Ken is going to pick me up from work."

Ken was a friend of hers and her cousins.

"We're all going to go to the funeral and then I'm going to call you when the funeral is over to see if you at home yet. And then, I'll get dropped off at your house," my sister said.

I was like, "Okay."

The next day, I went to the card game. I looked and saw what time it was and realized I needed to get home so I could start cooking before the kids got out of school. Since the funeral was during the day, and I had told Sirena I would make her some fish and stuff, I decided to head on home and start getting things together to start cooking. Where I was playing cards at was in a basement. My cell phone didn't have the greatest reception down there.

When I came out of the basement to go out to my car, my friend, Tammy, who called herself my sister, was like, "I'm coming over too. I'm going to come get me something to eat too."

Tammy and I were walking out to our cars at the same time. I looked at my cell, and it was telling me I had this many missed calls. Mind you, my phone never rung while I was in the basement. My cell showed I had 15 missed calls from my dad.

"Why is my dad blowing up my phone like a maniac?" I said. "What is going on?"

My car was parked on the street. There were cars all up and down the street because people weren't just coming to gamble and play cards. They were selling dinners there too and some people were coming to buy dinners. Me and Tammy had a long walk down the middle of the street to our cars. As we neared my car, the phone rang again. It was my dad.

I answered, "Like, dad, why do you keep blowing my phone up? What's going on?"

He screamed in the phone, "Your sister is dead!"

Just like that. I didn't understand.

"What? What? Wait, wait, what? What? Wait," was all I could say.

He said it again. I went down in the middle of the street. Not a, "Hi. Hello. It's an emergency. Get over here." He just screamed, "Yo sister is dead," in the phone to me and I collapsed right there in the streets. It was like my legs turned into noodles. It was a good thing somebody was with me because I probably would've gotten hit by a car. I was trying to process it. I was trying to understand what was going on.

"What do you mean? I just talked to her, what are you talking about?" I wailed. "Where is she? Where are you?"

In my mind, I couldn't process that. I had just talked to her the day before and she was fine. I'm a visual person. I have to be there, stand in it, visualize to fully grasp it. I guess my dad came to this realization.

He started screaming, "We're at General Hospital! The family is here at General Hospital! Your sister is dead."

He just kept saying that! I eventually hung up the phone on him. Before we could even load up to pulled off though, I was in the street distraught. Tammy had called to the house we were gambling at and told the people I was outside on the ground. You got to keep in mind, I was 300 and something pounds back then. She was telling them I was outside on the ground and needed help.

"Somebody gotta come pick her up. It's a family emergency. She needs help," Tammy pleaded.

Some of the people start coming out of the house and walked up the street to pick me up. I'm hollering and screaming in the middle of street. They were asking all kinds of questions as they helped me up while I grieved. Tammy had to respond for me.

They were like, "What's wrong? What's going on? Did she hurt herself?"

Tammy said, "Her dad just called and said her sister is dead."

Now, everybody understood what was happening. Since I couldn't drive myself, Tammy drove (although in a state of shock herself) and was trying to hold herself together to be able to hold me together. A couple of people and my girl Sidney got in the car with us and we drove down to the hospital. We were only about six minutes away from the hospital. Like I told you, the city is super small. But that six minutes felt like it took three hours to get there by the time we started driving.

When I get there, I see all my family outside. I knew what my dad had said was true, but I had to see that. I went inside. I heard her momma back there, and I can't even describe to you that moment. Her mother let out a scream that was unbelievable.

"I want to see her. Where's she at? Where's she at? I gotta see her," I demanded.

They had the family in the room with the chaplain. My sister's cousin was back there. They started trying to calm me down. I kept asking my questions. That was all I could say.

"Where's she at? Where's she at? What happened? What's going on? What happened?"

They said there was a real bad car accident. The car flipped over five times. Ken, the driver, was ejected from the car. Sirena, my sister, was killed instantly. That's why I don't so much trust seatbelts. They said it was the seatbelt that killed her. The jerk and snatch ended up snapping her spinal cord at the base of her neck from the seat belt's retraction.

"Oh, she didn't suffer," they said.

It still didn't lessen the pain of losing her. Sirena died instantly. She was five months pregnant. It was 30 days before her 18th birthday. That happened March the fifth. Her 18th birthday was in April.

She went to the funeral straight from work, and still had on her uniform. She never even got a chance to change clothes. They say, at the boy's funeral, they actually had an altar call. The pastor's message was prophetic.

"He said, 'Somebody here today is not going to make it to see tomorrow. So, I want you all to give y'all lives to Christ and say The Sinner's Prayer because there's somebody in here that's not going to make it to tomorrow. Tomorrow is not promised to any of us',' they said.

That was the message, but the guy, Ken, was drinking and got drunk at the funeral. He got into an argument with somebody. I guess he was beefing with that person over something. Still, first of all, it was disrespectful to carry on like that at somebody's funeral. That's not the time to cause a problem.

When dude he was beefing with pulled off, he started chasing the dude in the car. Ken, remember, was drunk. He blew a red light. A pickup truck hit them. Sirena never saw it coming. Investigators were wondering why there weren't any skid marks on the ground. They said as soon as the pickup truck made impact, the car Sirena nem were in went airborne. There won't be skid marks showing anybody tried to stop because the car went airborne instantly, flipped over five times, and stopped flipping because they slid into a telephone pole.

Sirena's cousins were in the car with her. They were all broke up. Sirena was in the back-passenger seat and her girl cousin was in the front passenger seat. She got all broke up. The boy that was in the back-passenger seat with my sister that rolled with them had a hole in his head the size of a fist. The driver, who was drunk got ejected? He broke his neck and died, but they brought him back at the scene. It was horrible. They all got messed up, but Sirena was the only one who died that day – her and her baby.

So, at that moment, I think I had a breakdown because the days following I couldn't eat or sleep. At the hospital standing with family learning this though, I went from asking where Sirena was getting angry that nobody would take me to her. Finally, when the doctor came in, they told me she wasn't even at the hospital. I was lost.

"What do you mean, 'She's not here?' Why the hell are we here then?" I snapped.

They said, "She died instantly. They didn't bring her to the hospital with the rest of the people. They took her straight to the coroner's office because she was dead."

You already know what happened next. I drove to the coroner's office – me, her mom, my dad, my brother and my friend. My dad and her mom were scared to go back there and see her. I didn't care what Sirena looked like; I was not going to rest until I saw her. They walked me to the morgue.

At first, they didn't let me go back there with her because they said she still had glass in her. Eventually, they had her laid out on the slab.. They had me in front of a window and they let the curtain up on the window. Her eyes weren't even all the way closed. Sirena just kind of looked like she was asleep, but her eyes just weren't all the way closed. She didn't look like she had any injuries. She didn't look like she had anything wrong. I petitioned to go in the room with her.

I said, "No. I want to hold her. I want to touch her. I want to hold her hand. I want to talk to her."

They let me go back there. That's when I saw what I couldn't see through the window. She had a little chunk of meat that was missing out of her chin. She had glass pieces in her face and in her arm. But, she still didn't look like she had gone through what she did. That's why my dad and her mom were scared to go see her. They thought she was gonna look mangled, but she wasn't. Sirena died from internal injuries.

That was the point where I had my breakdown. I went into a deep depression. I couldn't eat, I couldn't do anything for myself other than, at least, staying hydrated. My mother had to come stay with me because every time I went to go close my eyes, all I saw was Sirena lying on that slab. So, my mom felt like the doctors needed to give me something because I'd been up for days.

"They gotta give my baby something. She gotta sleep," Ma said.

She called my doctor's office and told my doctor what had been going on.

"I need you to give her some valium or give her something cause she needs to go to sleep," she told him when we got there. "She ain't even been eating. She be in a daze. She will drink water though."

They checked my pee and drew my blood. They checked everything because my mom was telling them what was going on with me and I was just sitting there like a zombie. I was looking at the doctor, but I couldn't hear nothing the doctor was saying. It was like a movie, like I was in a zone. For a short while, I couldn't see about my kids and I couldn't see about myself. I couldn't see about nothing. I didn't care about a bill. I didn't care about nothing.

That was when I found out that I was a diabetic. My blood sugar was 400 and something. So, they put me on medication for that gave me something to finally help me go to sleep. Then, we started making preparations for Sirena's and the baby's funeral. They were buried together.

After that, I kind of just went through the motions of life. I was depressed, but I just carried on. You know, when you're a mom, you gotta keep going. Right? So, I went through the motions. And, being in the abusive relationship didn't help at all. Five months later, things began getting better.

The great news was that my baby brother got accepted into Division One school he had made a verbal agreement with. Because he was getting ready to graduate from high school, we're excited that he's been drafted. We went to his graduation and had a pretty good time. Now that he had graduated and was accepted into that college for football, he was eager about the prospects up in PA. That summer, my baby brother was getting ready to go to the football camp before students returned and school started back.

In June, we celebrated my son G's birthday and the next month my daughters and mine. But, it wasn't the same because of the traumatic experience. Losing Sirena was traumatic for my kids too because they were really, really close to my sister. It was so traumatic for them that my daughter had to get counseling because she went to school and told the school that she wanted to cut herself with the glass that cut her auntie. When we had the funeral, that had not removed all the glass from Sirena. They did the best they could, but it was still some glass that was visible on her.

My daughter kept saying, "Mommy, why my auntie got glass in her? My auntie died from the glass?"

Since she thought Sirena died from getting cut by the glass, she went to school and expressed what she did. That was when her kindergarten teacher alerted met the fact that my little girl wanted to cut herself and die.

So, like I said, June we had G's birthday. That was the first birthday when my sister had been gone. In July, we had Tatiana a big birthday party. But, like I said, my baby was silently suffering from depression. If you are depressed, how can you help your depressed kids? At this time, Tatiana had turned five. In a state of shock, we couldn't believe that she even knew to think or say something like that.

When the teacher called me up there about Tatiana wanting to cut herself with the glass, I told her what happened to Sirena. Everybody knew about the news story and where it happened at, it was big news. So, when I said that my sister got killed leaving the funeral, the teacher remembered the accident because that's what creeped everybody out about it. You're leaving a funeral and you get killed. That was major buzz around our little city.

"That was my little sister," I told the kindergarten teacher. "We got the same father but different moms."

She was astonished.

"Wow. My heart goes out to your family," she said.

It finally made sense to her. She understood what Tatiana was talking about when she said she wanted to cut herself with glass. She realized my baby girl was saying she wanted to die the same way she thought her auntie had died, and she wanted to do it at this particular time because she wanted to see her auntie. My baby needed help. It was after that talk that we started getting Tatiana counseling at the school.

CHAPTER 11
The Great Injustice

Although she liked her home, my mom's duplex wasn't in the greatest neighborhood. There were a lot of drug sales going on and she would have to leave for work early in the morning. The dope dealers would be outside selling drugs in front of her house. Mostly, they were at this one particular house. The lady who lived in it was a crackhead. Her house was basically a flop house. The drug dealers would sell to anyone who walked in the yard or walked up to her door. Matthew was getting tired of it. Eventually, he couldn't rest knowing our mother was walking past this every morning. Those kinds of people and their customers were among the last people who needed to know the comings and goings from mama's house. Ma was even unnerved and got to where she couldn't sleep at night, not just because of the loud music pouring from the house across the street all times of night. So, one day, my brother got tired of it and started complaining. He went outside and told the dealers they had to leave the neighbor's house.

"Look, whatever y'all do, that's y'all. But, what y'all not going to be doing is selling these drugs in front of my mama's house. Y'all gone have to take this somewhere else," he told them

They left without incident. Matthew had a friend who lived next door. Rahim Bey was his best friend. Before Matthew had them to leave, Rahim's mama was getting into it with the dope dealers and the female neighbor all the time. Since they were side by side, my brother and his best friend were looking out for each other and their mothers 24/7. Matthew and his best friend were not new to getting on these dudes about selling drugs.

Well, the lady whose house it was told my brother, the day he expelled the dealers from her yard, that she was going to get him. She said he had to pay because he had no business trying to control her.

"You ain't stopping nothing from going on at my house! I won't stop at nothing until you regret the day you messed with me," she threatened as the dealers left and Matthew walked back into the house.

My brother quietly goes on about his business. Soon after, he leaves town for football camp. This was big news. Some of everybody was staying on top of his movements in the football arena. Our mom's neighbor wasn't one of them. She called the police and told the police that my brother came across the street and set her front door on fire. I know you want that sentence repeated to be sure you understood me correctly. Don't bother. There's more insanity to come.

The police went to my mother's house and was like, "Where's Matthew?"

My mom asked them why they were looking for him. That was when" one of the officers told her about the neighbor's claim.

"We got a police report filed by the lady across the street saying your son just set her door on fire," the policeman relayed.

My mom was like, "What the hell is she talking about? She made a police report saying Matthew set her door on fire? My son ain't even here! He's been at football camp for a week. He's in Pennsylvania."

The cops were floored and confused, "What?"

Mama said, "Yeah. He's been in Pennsylvania in football camp for a week. Let me tell you the real reason why she called and told that lie on my son. She told my son she was gonna get him."

That was when my mom filled the police in on everything that had happened the weeks prior when Matthew last had contact with the woman across the street. The policemen said they believed her because even they knew her house was a flop house and had noticed the activity had recently ceased.

"We used to be called over there all the time," one of them admitted. "We know what goes on over there. We know it's a flop house."

They said they were going to get her for making a false police report. Well, of course, nothing ever happened. This was at the end of August, beginning of September when that happened. Well, about two months later, there's an incident with this neighbor and my baby brother again. He was back from camp and it was around October or November. He wasn't playing football that fall because he had gotten injured and was still on crutches and wearing a cast. That didn't change her anger toward him for making her have to walk for her crack.

So, one night after Matthew got home, and he and the lady have an exchange of words before he goes inside the house. My mom was already in the house. It was late and everyone was getting ready for bed. Out of nowhere, they heard all these sirens, a helicopter hovering, and banging on the door.

"OPEN UP THE DOOR! Open up or we're going to kick it in," they yelled as they continued banging.

My mom got up out of her bed startled, confused and frightened. By the time she made it to the door, and they had never stopped beating on it and demanding it be opened, she was pissed.

"What the hell is going on?" She asked as she snatched the door open. "Why are y'all banging on my door like that?"

One of the police officers quickly spoke up.

"We're looking for your son. Where is he? We need him to come on out or we will come in and get him," he said.

"He's in there on the couch sleep,"

They started going through my mama's house. They were looking in trash cans and everywhere. They even took pictures of things as one officer was over by the couch telling Matthew to get up.

Mama said, "What in the hell is going on?"

So, they tell her that the neighbor across the street called the police and said my baby brother and his best friend next door came across the street with a knife and robbed her. She said they took her cordless phone and $100 in cash. She was obviously high.

Mind you, Matthew was sound asleep on the couch when the police came. On top of that, he was 300 plus pounds at the time and on crutches. The neighbor who lied on him weighed all of 50 pounds wet because she smoked dope.

After Matthew awakes, they put him in handcuffs and finished taking photos before hauling him off to jail. They arrested Rahim too. Both of them were charged with armed robbery. The police slapped on a lot of other crazy charges too, including kidnapping.

In the state of Ohio, if you're poor and Black, you're guilty until proven innocent. The kidnapping law says, if you move a person from one room to another against their will, that's considered kidnapping. Some kind of way, that fraudulent charge was put on my baby brother too. I can't even think of all the charges against they had again him and Rahim.

Mind you, I had just lost my sister. I was still grieving from that when my phone rang about this mess the neighbor created. They called me in the middle of the night, but my phone was on silent, so I didn't get the call until the next morning. I knew something was wrong when Ma started called my house at five o'clock in the morning, blowing my phone up. When I answered, she told me my baby brother was in jail.

"For what?" I asked her.

She filled me in on what the police said the lady across the street reported. Matthew's father still lived in Oklahoma. That's the man our mama left for messing with the neighbor. He had just gotten a big settlement right before Matthew was railroaded. He was an 18-wheeler driver and he had gotten into an accident. He ended up getting a six-figure settlement.

At first, Matthew had the public defender the court gave him. That's never good. With the seriousness of the crimes he was facing, that definitely wasn't good. When the indictment came back, that was when we knew he didn't stand a chance with a public defender. I call them public pretenders.

"There's no way he can have no public pretender on this case," I said.

Momma called Matthew's dad and told him, "I don't got no money. This boy is in trouble. His future is at risk and I'm going to need your help. Your son needs your help."

That was when his dad dropped the $10,000 on a lawyer. When I say every high-powered attorney was in there on the case, they were. He was well known. Matthew had already been on ESPN and long on the media's radar for his athletic talent. So, needless to say, his case was all over the news and in the papers. People could not believe it. They made him sound like a monster. They even said he was a part of a gang. We were all wondering what gang they were referring to. Matthew was all about football. He slept and breathed football until he got hurt.

"What gang is he a part of? A football gang?" We wondered.

My baby brother was never in a gang. He had never been in any kind of trouble, him nor the neighbor next door. The scene they had pictures of had been staged because. I mean, if somebody got a knife, why would they leave the knife they robbed you with sitting on your window seal outside your house? Who does that? She put that knife on the window seal outside her apartment. That knife didn't even bare their fingerprints.

I said, "Why would they rob her for a cordless house phone and $100?"

. Anybody with sense would have known that's not true. If he wanted to, that boy could have punched her and knocked her out or killed her ass. Plus, he was on crutches. Who can see a boy who's 300 plus pounds and nothing but solid muscle hobbling around on crutches robbing people and not say nothing about the crutches or cast in the description? Blatant lie but still upheld!

So, Matthew got the attorney and my mama's still a wreck. Now, she can't eat. She can't sleep. That's her baby boy. She knew how the system has done people there. So, she's worried halfway to death. She can't function. Her Graves' Disease is acting up.

My mother, right before Sirena got killed in a car accident, had gotten custody of Mitch's son, Cody. My middle brother was still living with me, and his son was living with our mother. Mitch was 20. And this was his second child. He already had a daughter.

They're the same age. They're less than a month apart. He had two girls pregnant at the same time.

. She needed her house back quiet because Mitch's baby boy was in there. Our mom had custody of Cody because his mother was on drugs and left the baby in the house by himself all night long while she went to go strip. The neighbors kept saying they heard the baby in there crying but they didn't hear nobody in here with the baby.

"We kept knocking on the door, knocking on the door, but kept hearing the baby crying. Nobody was coming to the door," they said.

So, they climbed through the window and saw that the baby had been in there all that time by himself. My brother wasn't together himself at this time. Thank God the people knew us and reached out to us. My family members lived in the same apartment complex as the girl. When the people saw Cody had been abandoned in the apartment, they went over to my cousins' house and then they called me. I went over there and got the baby and then we called the police from my mom's house.

When the police got there, they called children's services. So, the police came to my mom's house. They had to call in the emergency lady to come out that deals with children's services. Of course, ended up finding out my brother was on drugs and my nephew's mom was on drugs. She gave my mom temporary custody of my nephew while they sorted out a plan for what was going on.

My brother's dad dropped the 10,000 for the attorney because of the severity of the charges against Matthew. We got to court. They set their bonds at $1 million, like they had killed somebody. That meant they wanted 10% of $1 million to bail him out. Who you know that just got $100,000 laying around? I wished I did.

They kept going back and forth to court. The attorney got the bond reduced so we could try to get them out of jail. The lawyer argued fact that the boys had never been in any trouble. He pointed out how Matthew was a football star and was not a part of any gang. She even brought up the fact that this incident wasn't the first where the woman across the street lied on my brother to the police because he stopped the dealers from selling drugs in her yard.

The bond for Rahim and Matthew was reduced to $50,000. Ten percent of that is $5,000. We were able to get Matthew out while he continued going to court, thanks to his dad. Unfortunately, his co-defendant had to stay in jail because his family didn't have any money to get him out. If my brother's father wouldn't have had that accident, we wouldn't have had the money to get him out either.

We kept going back and forth to court, back and forth to court. Then, probably six months later in beginning of 2006, the prosecution finds out they really don't have a case. It was a new prosecutor trying to make a name for herself and she thought this high-profile case was her in. They got so desperate, they made serious blunders and oversights.

Trial was the goal. But, when they realized they really didn't have a case, they told my baby brother (right before the trial) that he can plead guilty on all charges and they would just give him a year in prison. Matthew wasn't biting. It had already been close to a year that he was dealing with this drama and he wasn't down for another year of it as heinous as the charges against him were.

"I'm not going to ruin my name! There's no way I'm gonna plead guilty to something I didn't do," he told us. "I'm going to the NFL. I am not going to cop no plea."

When they turned it down, all they said was that it was their final offer. A couple months later, the trial started. The trial lasted only six or seven days. The crazy part about it was the fact that the police department was testifying on my brother's behalf. The prosecution still pushed their defamation agenda and stood behind the false charges though.

They cleaned that crackhead up really good before they put her on the stand. She got caught in lies multiple times though. This was a high-profile case. All the top attorneys were in the courtroom, as well as other attorneys that were well known in Akron. They looked at this case so closely because they had someone who was a pro-athlete potential being charged by a female addict of a desperate and dumb robbery.

The whole thing was really a farce, but it was serious. Why would someone double the size of you rob you with a knife for a house phone and $100, then leave the knife outside on your window seal? If that person really wanted to rob you, they could've just snatched whatever they wanted, right? And, how can a person in a cast and on crutches rob anyone at knife point?

Matthew told my mom, "I know what I'm facing here. I'mma be okay."

I knew our family wouldn't be, especially not our mom. She was a wreck. She slipped towards deep depression herself at this point. She was still trying to hold it together for Matthew and for my nephew Cody, since she had him. We all knew, financially, our mother couldn't take care of Mitch's son. But, we couldn't let him go int the system. That's why I helped my mother even more during this time, because she was willing to go beyond her capacity and I needed to remind her that she has help.

"You gotta be the most stable person I know. They're going to feel like, because I'm so young and I've got kids of my own and the way my living situation is, they won't let me get him," I told her. "But, you get him, and I will help you take care of him. We've figured it out. You're getting him and I'll take care of him."

That was the agreement and that's what we did since Mitch and Cody's mom were still in the streets. I thought he and Rahim were in a good position with the crackhead doing so much lying. But, after the trial, my baby brother admitted his apprehension.

"I don't have a good feeling about it," he said. "I just feel like they're trying to railroad me."

In addition to the police, a number of people took the stand to testify on my baby brother's behalf. Matthew's dad even came to court, along with his woman and the rest of us. My baby brother had a lot of support in court. One of my favorite parts was when the police testified on my brother's behalf and openly discussed how the woman's house was a haven of drug activity. They said they had been called over there for several incidents.

"From beatings to the standard drug dealing, we've been to her house several times," one cop said. "Somebody had overdosed there one time, and I was one of the officers responding to that call."

They even brought up the fact that she had lied on Matthew before and their investigation revealed Matthew was gone to Pennsylvania at the time.

"He was attending to football camp and hadn't been in town for over a week," another policeman testified.

Instead of doing a trial by judge, Rahim and Matthew had a trial by jury. This jury wasn't listening to anything coming from the defense's side. These people already had their minds made up. They were prejudiced and held strongly to their bias. They were nowhere near being a jury of his peers. They determined guilt based on what they saw (their eyes) and felt (their fears), instead of what was said by witnesses (listening) and what the prosecution and defense presented (thinking). All but one of his jurors were White women. The other was a Black man. His accuser was a Black woman.

After the attorneys gave their closing arguments, the jury went into deliberation. We had been there all day already and had no idea how long it would take. We've all heard of these things dragging out so long to where jurors get sequestered. We were willing to wait as long as it took for Rahim and Matthew to be acquitted, but we expected the decision to be quick because of the preponderance of evidence showing their innocence.

Since none of our group had eaten anything, our family decided to go and grab something quick to eat. You gotta remember, my baby brother's co-defendant stayed in jail the whole time. When that happens, the inmate is escorted to court by correctional officers. Rahim also had a public defender. Considering all this plus the fact that the case was botched from the door, Rahim and Matthew shouldn't have ever went to trial together.

Their attorneys worked in the office. It was a conflict of interest. They didn't say anything about any of this. We didn't find out until after the sentencing. Of course, we didn't know about the law like that. That's why I tell people education is power. That's why I want money. I don't want money to be able to shine in front of people. I want money because of situations like this. I feel like, if we would've had more money and more resources, none of that would've ever happened.

When my brother and his friend got to court, my mother said she had a bad feeling time she saw the sheriffs escort Rahim in and sat him right beside Matthew. All those months of them going back and forth to court before, they never had more than two sheriffs to escort my brother's friend to court. This time though, they had a whole crew of them.

After the trial concluded and we broke to await the verdict. We placed or our orders and, just before they were ready, we got the call that the verdict was in. We got our food to go, grabbed our stuff, threw it in the car, and shot back down the street. We walked into the courtroom without a second more to spare.

The bailiff was saying, "All rise."

We walked in as the judge did. After the judge sat, everyone else in the courtroom sat down. Then, they called for Matthew to stand up.

"Will the defendants please rise?"

Matthew and his friend obeyed the judge's instruction. Then, the verdict was read by the jury foreman.

"On Count 1 of robbery, we find Matthew Pruitt & Rahim Bey guilty."

My mother almost collapsed. They didn't even get to the rest of the stuff before I knew what it would sound like.

"On Count 2 of kidnapping, we find the defendants guilty," the jury foreman said.

They got found guilty on every single charge, which they were facing up to 21 years on each charge. What she did was, basically, gave them 21 years for all of them but she ran it concurrently. That meant they each only had to do seven years. That was still seven years too many for two 19-years-old. It's a tragic sentence considering it was handed down on someone who had never been in trouble a day in his life. My baby brother didn't even have a traffic ticket.

I think that was the pinnacle of what changed my mom. She was no longer herself. She couldn't watch football or participate in any of the activities during football season. She used to be so passionate about football. She was even my baby brother's Peewee Football coach back in the day .Our mom was cold when it came down to football. She really could have been a professional football coach. She always called plays right. But, she lost her whole passion for football season after Matthew was done like that. She would be depressed and wouldn't be able to get out the bed. You couldn't turn on a football game on her TV.

"Don't even say the word 'football' in front of her," I had to warn people.

When they handcuffed my baby brother that day in the courtroom, I screamed and I hollered. You got to remember, all of this happened in a matter of a month. My baby sister is dead then my baby brother got sentenced to prison.

"I know this is really racism! He's a boy," I cried.

They railroaded him and his co-defendant. These were young boys. They were 19 years old and ain't been in no trouble. Then, to think that this person that told that lie on them! Now, I was really feeling like I needed to do this check stuff because my baby brother needed money for this jail stuff and we just didn't have stacks of money sitting around like that.

CHAPTER 12
Getting Desired Justice

Now, my brother Mitch done flipped the hell out because our baby brother done got railroaded and sent to prison. My middle brother (the one whose son my mother was taking care of) lost it! He was going around saying he wanted to go and kill the lady. We literally lost it and went on a rampage. He flipped, mentally, because our mother raised us to always look out for each other.

"If something happens to me, all y'all got is each other," she told us all our lives.

I have other siblings through my dad. Our baby brother has other siblings through his dad. But, we're the only siblings our middle brother has. That's why he lost it when they did our baby brother like that. He just flipped out and was trying to figure out something to do so he could go to jail to protect our baby brother. That was how connected they were.

My middle brother was the one, as you know, that caused the most trouble. He's been in that life and was in the game. My baby brother didn't do nothing like that lifestyle. All he was concerned with was football. My baby brother was supposed to be the football star. My middle brother was just out there, girl. That middle child! It ain't no middle ground with him. He was always the hot-headed one since we were kids anyway. I love my brother dearly, but he really off the hook

Anyway, the next thing I knew, the mother of Mitch's baby girl called my phone saying my brother wanted to talk to me. She said my brother needed to talk to me, but he didn't want to do it on the phones. She told me he would call me from someone else's phone and for me to get a number for him to call me on that's not my phone.

"Why I gotta go through all that? He can just call me on my phone," I told her.

She went ahead and told me, "No, no, no. They got a warrant out for his arrest for robbery."

Mitch was angry about what happened to Matthew still. So, he robbed the guy my brother he was buying his weed from. He went over there to Ray The Weed Man's place and took money and weed at gunpoint. Although he was saying he wanted to go to jail, he admitted that he really thought the dealer wouldn't turn him in.

He said, "The boy said, 'I don't care if I go to jail for selling. We can all go to jail. I'm telling.' That fool called them for real."

Now, the police were looking for my middle brother with a vengeance. He lived with me, as you know. Some of everybody knew that. Guess whose house they went to with sirens and banging on the door looking for Mitch? Yep. Straight to our mama's house. Mama was now really two seconds from a nervous breakdown.

While Mitch was out on the run, my dad got indicted. He had already been in so much trouble and went to prison for checks, and they were after him about checks again. They were trying to hit him with the financial crimes RICO Act because he had already been in trouble for financial stuff before. When they came trying to get my dad under the Racketeer Influenced and Corrupt Organizations Act, they came with tunnel vision. This will come back up later. But, at this time, my dad is indicted while my middle brother was on the run.

Ma held on by a thread. The father of her first child may be going back to prison. Her oldest son was on the run. Her baby boy was in prison for crimes he didn't commit. I, her daughter and oldest child tried to not worry her but knew she was still worried about me and my kids too.

She had a lot on her. Imagine your child, the one you thought was going to be the one God used as your saving grace, getting convicted of a slew of serious crimes he did not commit and there was nothing you could do about him being gone. Now, imagine cops coming to your house a couple of weeks later looking for your middle child to take him away for something he did. Top that with health issues and other life things going on. My heart broke even more for my mother during this period.

They had that warrant out for Mitch for a few months. It took them a while to find him. He was out on the run for at least 60 days. It could have been 90 days because I remember how worried I was that they would just shoot him on the spot because they'd been searching for so long, talking about he was armed and dangerous. Mama was trying to get Mitch to turn himself in.

I said, "Look, I'll take you down there so you can turn yourself in."

He was like, "Naw. Un un. I ain't turning myself in."

He just went on a binge. He was constantly getting drunk and staying high. He couldn't function. I mean, how do you live on the run? That ain't no life. He started popping ecstasy pills, drinking, snorting cocaine, smoking weed, and doing everything you could possibly imagine, probably with the exception of meth and heroin.

. I was worried that now he was going to kill himself doing all those drugs like he was doing. I didn't want my brother to have no overdose and end up killing himself.

So, I just was praying to God every night, "Lord, please don't let the police kill him. Let the police capture my brother without harming him. Please don't let him overdose. Please just let the police get him and take him in peacefully."

I was praying every prayer possible. Anything I could think to mention in my prayers, I would. Next thing I know, I get a phone call from his daughter's mom saying that the police got him. He had called his daughter's mom, I guess when they were taking him into custody. In the midst of him being on the run, we find out he got another baby on the way.

His son and his daughter were like three weeks apart. My nephew Cody and my niece Ariel both were born in at the end of 2004 I was 25 at this point in the story, so Mitch's kids are around two years old. He had a new baby on the way and was just arrested after being on the run all those months.

He told the mother of his daughter they were taking him into custody and to come and get his stuff. The whole time, nobody had no money to get him out on bond like they did Matthew. My middle brother, like I said, all Mitch got is me and my mom. He had to go back and forth to court from inside the county jail.

I would go down there every week. I'd put money on his books so that he could have commissary. I wanted to be sure he knew he had an outlet, a support system or whatever you want to call it. The county jail was only 10 minutes from my house. Sometimes, I would go down there twice a week.

I was getting ready to be 26. This had been the worst year of my life. My birthday was coming up in July. Like I had told you, I was involved somewhat in the check game already. I'd just tell them how they can do it better and what to do, and they would give me a cut.

My middle brother had always looked at me like I'm his mother. So, my brother started asking me what he should do.

"Do I take a plea bargain? Do I take it to trial? What do I do?" He questioned.

Because his situation was a little bit different, I told him flat out, "I can't believe they really trying to make a case stick behind a supposed drug robbery,"

But, the boy that he robbed was White. That was why they were making so much noise about it. Mitch went back and forth to court or a couple months. They wanted to do a speedy trial. He had a public defender. So, Mitch asked the judge could he come in her chambers and bring me with him before he got sentenced.

They took a break and they let us all go into the judge's chambers. We talked about options and I told her how our baby brother had already been railroaded, how young he was, and how I didn't want that to happen to my middle brother. I talked to her about my sister that had passed right before my baby brother was wrongfully imprisoned and how I believed Mitch had a breakdown when Matthew was sent up the river like that.

"Honestly, I did not have a lot of faith in the judicial system," I admitted.

I told the judge about our mother's debilitating diseases and everything we were dealing with behind that. The toll the stress of these situations with her boys was evident. I explained to her how these situations were literally breaking her heart and killing her at the same time.

"She's not in the best of health. She has his son, her grandson, and I'm trying to assist her the best I can with the baby," I said. "But, you know, I want him to not spend the rest of his life in jail. He can be rehabilitated and come out here and be a productive citizen in society and be able to look after his own children."

The judge was like, "How old are you?"

I told her I was 25 going on 26.

She said, "I'm blown away by you. You are so young but, at the same time, you have an old soul. It's like you out here fighting for everybody."

And, I said, "I am. Because, if nobody fights for them, whose gonna fight for them?"

After we took that 15-minute recess, we came back for sentencing. They would up be giving it to him tough. Our cousin, his co-defendant, got it too because they both were together when it happened. They got six years in prison.

The officers took Mitch away from the courtroom right then and there straight to the county jail. After about a week or two after he was sentenced, they got him and transported him in the middle of the night to the correctional facility. And then, guess what happened.

My brothers wound up at the same prison together. It was a mission accomplished for Mitch. When the officials found out they were brothers, they put them together. Because they don't have the same last name, they didn't know before it was brought to their attention that they were actually blood brothers. My baby brother has his daddy's last name and my middle brother has my daddy's last name.

My mother wrote a letter to them letting them know they had the same mother and she would like to be able to visit them both at the same time. When we submitted that request, we also asked that they not be moved further than two hours away so that my mother could continue to visit them both while they served out their sentences. We explained that she couldn't drive, because of her health problems.

They ended up moving both of them. They put both of my brothers the Mansfield Correction Facility, which was about an hour and seven minutes from where we lived. At that point, I had two brothers to support in jail. I was taking care of my health and my own kids. And, I was helping my mama take care of her health and my nephew.

I was like, *What more can I do? I'm tapped out.* I was literally mentally and physically drained. I was overwhelmed. I wasn't in the best of health because I was a diabetic. I had gone from pills to insulin. I was still with Zee, but I was going through separation anxiety.

One day, after I came back from visiting my brothers, it all came down on me. See, I would drive down and go see them every week because I needed to see them with my own eyes to make sure they were okay. I was seriously going through separation anxiety. I wasn't used to being without my brothers like that. I would go and sit with them and do everything we could do. When I left, I would be crying like a baby the whole drive back. I was literally making myself sick.

"No! You can't go every week like this," my mama told me.

I still went back to see them every week. I still sat with them and did everything we could. Then, one day, she called me and told me she wanted me to come over to her house. She said she had something she needed to talk to me about.

"Okay," I said. "Well, once I get the kids out of school, I'll just come to your house afterwards. As a matter of fact, what you got over there to cook?"

She was like, "Actually, I'm looking through my deep freezer now trying to find something."

I said, "Well, I'll stop by the grocery store before I go get the kids. I'll bring something over there and then we could all just have dinner together."

I was still trying to keep her together mentally, and I wasn't even together mentally. She was trying to do the same thing for me. But, that's my mom.

CHAPTER 13
Change Comes Knocking

Ma had finally gotten a promotion at her job. She was now a house manager at a mental health home, and she was making more money. Now, God has always shown my mother stuff in her dreams. Since I was a little girl, she has always seen things in her dreams. At her request, I went by her house that day after grabbing up some groceries. Time I got there, she didn't hesitate cutting straight to the chase.

"I know I never asked you, and I told you that never would," she said. "So, this is what I'm going to say to you. Whatever you're doing, you need to stop. I had a dream last night that the police had your whole house surrounded. I don't know what it is. You the only one I got left. So, whatever you're doing, I need you to stop."

I just said, "Okay."

About 30 days went by. After that, we had dinner together. I was going over there every day to check on her and my nephew and doing stuff with them. Two weeks after that conversation with Ma, I started getting to the point where I couldn't sleep at night. I didn't know what it was, but I couldn't sleep worth nothing. I had just turned 26 so I'm 26 now. Her words kept playing in my head.

"Whatever you're doing, you need to stop it."

I started putting in job applications. Life had already shown me that, when my mama tells me something God showed her in her dream, 90% of the time she'd be right. I had already decided I was ready to change my life. But, that night I told God that I wanted to get out of that relationship with Zee and the check game all together.

"That's not me. I don't want to be in it anymore. It is debilitating and draining," I told my Lord. "I don't want to be in that life. I don't want to be in this relationship no more. It's not healthy."

My kids were getting older and so was I. I needed to find ways to minimize risk and loss to them. They needed to be around something that was positive. I kept telling God I wanted to get out of it, and I was hoping a couple of those job applications panned out. There was one job that I really, really wanted. I was so happy when they reached out to me and asked me could I come in for a job interview.

They said, "Can you come to the interview in two days at 10 a.m.?"

I told them, "Sure I can!"

I woke up the morning of the interview excited about the job. I wanted a job that I could take care of my family off what it pays, and this one was a good prospect. As I took my shower upstairs, I kept saying to myself that I heard something that sounded like knocking but I didn't think much of it. I just screamed out for somebody to answer the door. I went ahead and finished showering, then I put on some clothes and headed to the basement to finish washing before I left for my interview.

I heard the knocking again. Whoever it was kept knocking. Nobody in the house ever answered the door. The knocking stopped as I loaded the clothes in the dryer. The time was creeping closer for me to leave, so I rushed out of the basement so I could grab my keys and resume to head to the interview. When I opened the door, I saw a card from the Financial Crimes Department fall down.

On the card, the detective had written, "Tiffany, we need to talk."

My heart fell to my stomach. All I could think of was my mama saying for me to stop whatever I was doing. I went back in the house and told Zee the policer had been here and that was who we heard knocking on the door.

"How do you know?" Zee asked.

I said, "Because they left a card in the door saying for me to call them."

I was thinking, *What do we need to do? What are we gonna do?* I decided to go on to my job interview and then call them after the interview was behind me. After my interview was over, I went ahead and called the detective that had come by the house. The police told me to come to the station to answer some questions. I immediately called Aunt Renee, my dad's sister on the force. I told her about how the detective from the Financial Crimes department came by the house and said they needed me to come down and talk to them.

"You can do one of two things. You can come down and talk to them or you could tell them you don't want to talk without an attorney," she said. "If you decide to come down and talk to them, tell them absolutely nothing because they're fishing and that's it."

I was still dressed up from the job interview, so I went on down to the police station, went up to the 6th Floor, and asked for the detective that was on the case. A man and woman came out and took me in the back room. The female detective was the one that had come to my house. The male detective was her partner. They pulled out a recorder and they put this thick book on the table. It had a picture of my dad on the front of it.

When they opened the book, my picture was on the first page. The following pages had pictures of different people. Some were pictures of people I realized I knew, and some of the people I didn't know. They had pictures of a lot of people in this book, even a picture of my sister who is now deceased. They had Zee's picture and Zee's daughter's picture too. I didn't know most of the people in the book because they were people that were doing stuff with my dad. Many of them were drug addicts that I didn't know.

"We've been watching y'all the last two years," the male detective said. "You've been under investigation for a long time."

We've been under investigation for the last two years? I knew that wasn't true because they didn't know until the last minute

142

that my dad was my dad because I didn't have his last name. If you looked at us on a photo though, we look just alike. Everybody always be like, "If yo daddy put on a wig, y'all would be able to pass for sisters."

They didn't know that my father was my father and, like my aunt told me, they were fishing. They had brought in everybody whose pictures they saw in that book. They brought them in first for questioning, and then brought me in last. The people in the book that were affiliated with me and Zee didn't know my daddy nem, And, the people affiliated with my daddy nem didn't know me and Zee nem. Our people didn't know each other because we never did nothing with them.

The detectives were trying to put two and two together because they wanted to hit us with the RICO Act and make it federal because of how much money the stores lost. They were really hoping to make a case for family money laundering. But because me and my father had never committed a crime together, they couldn't do it. They had recorded their interrogations of everybody.

"Do you know Tiffany Trammell?" The police would ask.

My dad's people would be like, "Who is Tiffany Trammell? We don't know who that is. Who is that?"

So, they showed them the picture they had of me and asked, "Have you ever been with you guys when you guys were doing stores?"

They were like, "No. I ain't never seen or heard of no Tiffany Trammell."

Of course, we did not know each other. I wasn't hanging around no bunch of drunks, junkies and crackheads. Anyone watching me for a long time would know that. The detectives, even though I looked like my dad, still couldn't put the two together. They went through the same thing when they asked my people if they knew a Mitch Holloway.

The people that knew me were like, "Naw, we don't know no Mitch Holloway."

The detectives were like, "Are you sure you don't know Mitch Holloway?"

They said, "Yes. I ain't never seen or heard of him before right now with you."

The police say they had been working on this case for two years. But, they still couldn't piece the puzzle together. They had been put in the case together, but they still couldn't piece the put the puzzle together. The problem came in when one of the ladies doing the checks decided to go off on her and tried to do it so she wouldn't have to give anybody a cut of her money. She got caught because she didn't know what she was doing, then she got scared and started talking about the people she was doing it with. That's how the investigation started in the first place. That came out of their own mouths.

"We would have never even had a clue if this lady wouldn't have come forward and started putting the puzzle together for us," they bragged.

No wonder they were clueless. She didn't even have the whole puzzle. She overlooked the main principle. You don't tell the people everything you know because then they don't need you anymore. You see what I'm saying? So now, you done went off on your own and you don't get a cut of nothing. That's why she got caught. And, guess who she called to get her dumb self out of jail.

Me! And then, she told on me. She wasn't going to get no more than probation because it was a Felony 5 financial crime where she could have gotten probation and paid restitution. When I went in to talk to them, they tried to scare me with their talk about felonies. But, I had nothing to give them that they wanted.

"We gonna charge y'all with felony money laundering, wire fraud, conspiracy, the whole gamut," the female detective said. "Who is this man? We know you know him."

I was like, "Come on y'all. Cut the games."

They knew that was my daddy. He and my auntie had the same last name. My auntie worked at the police department and they knew that was my auntie. They knew my dad was her favorite brother. They didn't like Renee in the police department anyway. This was more personal than what it was about cleaning up crime. This was a personal jab at her because they were trying to get her job from her anyway. They had tried to get her under some kind of investigation.

When all of your brothers are criminals and you're the damn police, other people try to make it bad for you. But you can't control them. Those are your older brothers. You see what I'm saying? They were trying to make it hard for her. This was more than just the average case they were trying to pull together. This was a personal vendetta.

I said, "Certainly y'all know that I would know my own father. Please spare me the humility."

So, they were like, "You know, we just indicted him."

Remember, I had told you how my dad got indicted when my middle brother was on the run. When my brother caught his case, they pulled my dad over and he thought it was just a regular traffic stop. He figured it was something like failure to use a turn signal. They pulled him over and arrested him because they had a warrant for his arrest. He didn't even know. So, my dad was out on bond going back and forth for checks and I was going back and forth to court with him.

Right after that, the next thing I know, my Auntie Renee called me and said, "Look, I'm just telling you, they drafted a warrant for your arrest. So, whatever you're going to do, you better do it."

I guess the detectives didn't like it when I went down there and, after talking to all those people before me, I showed them nothing and they had nothing. I basically told them to do their jobs. After all, I went there because they had questions not because I did. They got on my nerves asking the same questions over and over about people I didn't know and that they knew didn't know me and pretending like they didn't know Mitch Holloway was my daddy.

"You told me you had questions for me about something that I did. Don't question me about nobody on no picture. You already know that I know my father, because that's my daddy. Now, the rest of these people I don't know," I said. "As for the people I do know, you ask them what they did. If you want to question me about something I did, the floor is yours."

They kept pissing me off. So, I enacted my American privilege and pursued my happiness.

"This interview is over! Am I under arrest?" I huffed.

"No, but we will be in touch," the female detective said.

I got up and walked out. They had all that on the recording. They used that against me later in court. When I left, I went straight to my mother's house. I told her what happened, and she just busted out crying.

She was like, "I knew it! I knew it, I knew it, I knew it!"

Remember, I told you how I saw pictures of Zee and his daughter in the book. They were the next ones to be interviewed. They didn't call none of us in there together. When they went down for questioning, I didn't go with them. I let them go by themselves.

They were the last pieces of the puzzle for the detectives. Everybody else had already been questioned.

This was the thing though. When they questioned my dad after he was arrested, they never asked him anything about me. They asked my people and his people about me. So, after they talked to Zee and Zee's daughter, about 10 days went by. I became nervous. I was a wreck. I didn't know what I was going to do if the worst happened. I started pulling all my money out the bank.

I told my mom, "Go get a bank account. I'm going to have to just put all my money in your bank account cause I don't know what these people about to do."

I was 26 by now and school had already started back for the kids. It was cold outside; I remember we had on jackets. So, all this was going on around October 2006. They went and I had to make the best of it that I could. About 10 days later, I saw my aunt's number pop up on the phone. I wasn't in Akron, but I was only about 20 minutes away.

That was when she said to me, "They just drafted a warrant for your arrest. Whatever you gone do, you need to do it. And, you cannot be seen in any vehicle that has your name on it."

So, what I did was called my best friend at that time, Sherry. I also happen to have an aunt named Sherry.

I said to my best friend, "Sherry, my Aunt Renee just called me and said they just put out a warrant for my arrest."

She was like, "What?"

Sherry worked at Chrysler. She was my straight-laced friend. She wasn't going to do nothing wrong.

She said, "What? Wait a minute. What the hell?"

I was like, "Look, I need you to get me a hotel room cause I can't get it in my mama's name. I can't get it in nobody's name that they know I am related to. I need to get a hotel room under your name, and I need to drive your extra car because there are some things I need to do. They're going to be looking for my vehicles, so I can't drive them."

Sherry was one of my dearest friends. She left work to get me straight. We'd fall out along the way sometimes. But, at that moment, I found out who really had my back because my back was against the wall. She left work, called her twin sister, and told her to meet us where they met me at. They took me out to a little suburb outside of where I lived and got me a hotel room. Sherry gave me her car and got in the car with her twin. I hurried up and got to handling my business because I didn't know how much time I had since they had just drafted the warrant. But, I knew they were coming.

My aunt had let me know that they had put a warrant out for all our arrests – Zee's, Zee's daughter, and mine – and we all lived in the same house. I went home and we started packing suitcases. I kissed my babies and got on my way. It broke my heart to leave my kids under those circumstances, but I was at least happy they were at my house. School had let out at 2:30. My cousin was staying there with me and Zee and the kid at that time because I told my cousin what was going on, I gave him a stack of money, and I told him I had to go.

"I've got to go. I cannot be here because I know they're coming," I said. "I don't want them to take me into custody and I'm stuck having to try to get me an attorney from inside of jail. I want to be able to turn myself in with an attorney."

He understood. So, I called my great-aunt. The one I told you named me and taught me about God. She's the same one that I went to live with when she was sick, and I was 10. Like I said, one thing I knew, if I were ever in trouble, she had my back. I need to talk to her. I need her to hear her voice.

I said, "I can't be on the phone long. I don't know if they going to be trying to tap my phone or what. I'mma get another phone and I'mma call you."

It was my friend Sherry who went and got me another phone that I could call people on. Once she gave me the phone, I called my aunt and my mom to tell them my plans.

"I need you to go to the house with Ray and the kids," I told my aunt.

I told my mom that my Aunt Renee called me and said the police had a warrant for my arrest. I filled her in on how I was already packing my stuff and leaving until I found myself an attorney.

"I'm not telling you where I'm going," I explained to my mom. "So, if they do come to your house looking for me, you will be telling the truth when you say you don't know where I am."

CHAPTER 14
Wandering The Wilderness

My mom was on that phone balling her eyes and throat sore.

She was like, "No! I told you and told you! You should have been away from that situation. I had been praying for God to get you out of that!"

She was going on and on. I had to shift her focus.

I said, "Mom, this is not the time. I got to figure out what I need to do and what's best for me. This ain't the time though to talk about what we should have done, what we could have done."

She agreed, "We can't change it now. All we can do is face it and keep the faith."

I got off the phone with my mom and started calling attorneys then the family members that knew what was going on and knew good attorneys for stuff like this. I mean, some of them had attorneys that got them out of major stuff. They were texting me attorneys' numbers left and right. I was staying in a hotel, but I would call my mom to let her know I was alright. When she would pick up the phone, I would say, "I'm okay," and hang up. I wanted to keep the calls as brief as possible. I was running for about two weeks.

Sometimes, all I would say is, "Don't worry. It's all going to be okay. It's all gonna work out. Everything will be alright."

I didn't know if the phone line was bugged or what, and I didn't want to risk my location being traced or getting my mother in any trouble. I called my great-aunt who had my babies and I had a quick heart-to-heart with her. I told her the same thing I told my mom.

"It's all gonna work out. It's gonna all be good."

Well, after the first week I was gone, my great-aunt was in the house with the kids and my cousin. They were in there and watching TV or whatever before they had to put the kids to bed. My great-aunt was in there watching church on the TV after the kids went to sleep. My cousin was up there playing the video game. They said they heard loud knocking on the door.

"BOOM, BOOM, BOOM, BOOM, BOOM! And I was like, 'Who is it?' They were the Akron Task Force, the police department," my grandmother's sister told me.

She said she opened the door and was astonished. She said she looked down the street, both ways, and she couldn't believe it. Police had the house surrounded. Blue lights were everywhere, and as far as she could see. They had the house surrounded and the street was blocked from one end to the other. No one could come in or go out. This was what my mother saw in her dreams.

Cops were everywhere, my great-aunt said. After they asked her all these questions about who she is and where I was, she told them she was my aunt and asked why they were looking for me. That was when she said they asked her if she knew where Zee's daughter, Zee and I were again, and they told my great-aunt why they were looking for us three. My great-aunt told them she didn't know where we were but that wasn't good enough for them.

She said they went through my whole house, even checking the attic. Remember, my cousin was upstairs in his bedroom. So, the police went upstairs going through my room, going through my kids' rooms, going through my drawers, looking all in the basement and stuff. My great-aunt said she reminded them that the kids were in there asleep.

"I'd so appreciate it if y'all can be as quiet as possible because I don't want you to scare them out of they sleep," my great-aunt told the police officers.

So, they quietly finished up. But, not before going in and questioning my cousin. caught. He called that phone I was using after they left.

I had an Expedition truck and a purple Grand Prix. I parked both of my vehicles in the driveway because I knew they were going to be looking for them. My cousin told me the police were questioning him about the cars being there still.

"They said, 'Well her cars are here,' and I told them, 'Well, she ain't here and I can't make her be here.' That's when they asked, 'Where is she?' And I told them 'Hell, I don't know. Y'all the police. Ain't y'all supposed to know'," my cousin said.

Our great-aunt said they were questioning my cousin for a minute. It was my cousin who told me about how they were searching through my whole house and telling him how they had a warrant for my arrest. He said they told him that I better turn myself in because if they have to catch me first, it was going to be worse for me. That was when I amped up my search for an attorney and I found one. A great one at that too.

Even though my relationship with Zee was pretty much over at this point, I still wanted to offer any help I could while I masterminded my way to get out of the relationship. I knew I couldn't have a paid attorney and they have a public defender if it was going to work out for all of us. This was really my way of getting out and not looking back. So, I called the attorney, went to his office, and retained him for all three of us. He called the detective on the 6th Floor and told him he was going to be bringing all three of us in the next day so we can turn ourselves in. They set up a time for us to be at the police station, and they hung up.

"This is the thing. You don't have to stay. We're gonna walk you in and out," he said. "You won't go in a cell. You're gonna get fingerprinted and you're gonna get your pictures taken. Then, they'll process it and we'll get you a signature bond since you've never been in trouble before."

That was all good for me, but Zee had been in trouble before. I wondered if Zee could get a signature bond too.

"Is everybody gonna get a signature like me?" I asked him.

He said no.

"Since I'm all yall's attorney, I'm having them process you first because you've never been in trouble. Anytime you have a co-defendant, whenever they get one, they get the other so I'm having them to process yours first. That means they will get a signature bond because you got a signature bond. Their signature bond may be higher if they've offended, but your signature bond will probably be a $5,000 signature."

I called my mother and my friend Sherry. I had my mother to meet my friend Sherry to give her the money for the retainer. Then, I had Sherry to meet me at the lawyer's office with the money. I remember Sherry took off work to help me handle this. She brought the money my mom sent for all three of us that Monday. We three were already at the attorney's office and immediately signed the paperwork right after I paid him. That was when he had us to follow him and he took us down to turn ourselves in.

"Y'all can really drive if y'all want to because you're not gonna have to stay," they attorney said. "You could also have somebody drop you off. I don't know how long it's going to take, so they probably would not want to stay."

So, we followed him on down. We walked in, they took our pictures and our fingerprints, and they walked us over to the courtroom. The courthouse was connected to the police department, so the walk was a short one. They just walked us across the bridge to the courthouse and when we got to the courtroom, the judge said sign the $5,000 signature. They took us back downstairs and it just was kind of a waiting game for everybody's paperwork to get processed. As they were letting us go home, our lawyer said for us to meet him back at his office the next Monday.

"By then, the indictment should be in because these are just the original charges. The actual indictment that goes before the grand jury takes about a week," the attorney said. "Let me have y'all come back next week on Monday. By then, the indictment showing the charges should be in and, at least, we'll know what we're facing."

That was a Monday, and the rest of that week I was a wreck. Even though I was back home with my kids and handling things, I couldn't quite get into the swing of things because I really was an absolute wreck because I didn't know what to think about my situation or future. I'd never been in nothing like this before. I didn't know what to think. I went over to my mom's. I went to my aunt. I went to my great-aunt.

My great-aunt was like, "Look, I've been petitioning God to get you out of that situation."

I knew that sometimes, He alone, is the help we need. I also knew my mom was trying to stay positive but, at the same time, she was trying to tell me why she believed I was going through what I was facing.

She said, "I believe it's a bigger purpose to why all of this is happening. But it had to happen."

So, I was like, "Okay."

That Monday, we went down to the attorney's office. On the ride down, Zee's daughter and I weren't very chatty. I think we all had a lot on our minds. At least, I know I did. I had a lot of uncertainty still remaining about this whole mess I was in. When we got to the attorney's office, he quickly put everything in perspective.

"Hi. I'mma need y'all to sit down," he said.

CHAPTER 15
Accused & Betrayed

Before we went to the lawyer's office that Monday, we knew the initial indictment was already weighty. It was for passing bad checks and receiving stolen property. Zee's daughter and I were each looking at a Felony 5.

"I need to tell y'all. Now that the indictment has come back, in all of my years of being in this town, I've never seen a document like this in my life," the attorney said. "I usually see indictments like this in federal cases, not in state court. That's why I'm kind of worried. I don't know if the feds are gonna pick this up. Your Felony 5 is now a Felony 2, 3 and 4 per the RICO Act."

With the Felony 2, we were each looking at a minimum of 2 to 8 years. They tied it with the RICO Act because of the number of co-defendants involved. When drug dealers get hit with the RICO Act, they get life in prison.

He even said, "God is really working on yall's behalf for y'all to even been able to get a signature bond to get out last week because the people in the indictment said their whole business got messed up."

One of the companies involved was Sherwin Williams There were three stores they said that went out of business because of us. What they were doing was writing checks for stuff like paint and wallpaper and taking it back to get cash over a period of time. There were a couple of banks on there saying they felt like we were a menace to society because of how much money their banks had lost. I mean, it was just nuts.

So, at that moment, we started going to court and had to determine whether we wanted to do a speedy trial. Our lawyer said he needed to get the recording from the police department so he could find out what all was said by people about us.

"I have to do something called the motion of discovery," he said. "We gotta find out who's telling them what, so we know how to attack the case. What I want you to do to make it look better for all y'all is I need y'all to go get a job somewhere. I don't even care if it's at McDonald's. I need y'all to go get a job ASAP."

So, all three of us started putting in job applications that same Monday after we left the attorney's office. The love relationship Zee and I had was basically over. It wasn't completely over yet, but this is what really wrapped it up. I wound up interviewing and getting hired on the spot for a job at Dish Network. They're kind of like Direct TV. My mom always said I could sell water to the ocean. They offered me top pay and bonuses. I was working up in Canton, Ohio – which was about 20 minutes from where we lived. I started working full-time right away. One day while I'm at work, I got a phone call from my attorney saying we desperately needed to talk.

"It's imperative that I speak to you, like yesterday," he said. "I don't need you to bring anybody with you. I just need you to come and not to tell anybody that you're coming to see me."

I did like he said. I didn't tell my mom, my great-aunt, my Aunt Renee, Zee, Zee's daughter, nor my friends. I left work early to be sure I caught the attorney before his office closed. When I got there, he was wrapping up with his client. The receptionist offered me some water and snacks while I waited. After the client he was with left, my attorney opened the door to his office and this man's face was blood red as he had me to enter his office.

"I need you to sit down and I need you to take a deep breath," he said as I walked past him, and he closed the door.

I was like, "Okay."

He said, "We have a problem."

I sat down and said, "What's the problem?"

He said, "As you know, I'm your attorney, I'm Zee's attorney, and I'm the attorney for Zee's daughter because you retained me for everybody. But going through the paperwork, preparing for court, and going through the motion of discovery, we learned that Zee and Zee's daughter signed a paper saying that they will testify against you if you go to trial."

I was floored.

"What the hell?" I exclaimed. *I'm the one who paid for your attorney and you plot against me? Really?* "Wait. What?"

He calmly replied, "Do you want to see the paperwork?"

That was when he broke things down for me.

"This is a conflict of interest. I can't represent all three of you," he said.

I was sitting in his office in a state of shock. I wouldn't even know nothing about none of this if it wasn't for him discovering this. I was beyond livid. I was seeing blood. So, I called my mama.

I told her, "Ma, I'm already out on bond for this case. But, if somebody don't get those people out my house, I'm gonna be in jail for murder."

My mom asked me what was going on. I told her what the attorney told me.

"That's why I didn't call you from my cell phone," I admitted.

"I almost didn't answer the phone cause I didn't know whose number this is," she said.

I then told her about how the attorney had called while I was at work and that I had left work early.

"I'm down here meeting with the attorney right now. He called me while I was at work and said it was an emergency. I needed to come today and not to bring anyone with me and not to tell nobody I was coming."

She was like, "I knew it, I knew it, and I knew it. This idiot has been your downfall from the beginning."

Mama called my cousin and filled him in on everything since he was staying with us. He made it a point to handle up on things before I made it home. Zee and his daughter were home at the time because neither of them had gotten a job.

"Look, y'all my people. But, that's my cousin," he told them. "Everybody got to go, and I mean right now!"

To make sure they got the point, he started packing their stuff for them.

"You ain't gotta to go your mama's house, Zee, but you and your kids gotta get the hell up outta here," he said.

They started packing really fast. That was my way of being released from all of that. When I got home, there was a peace there that I had never felt before. I don't know if it was because I was still somewhat in a state of shock or whether it was because a big burden had been lifted off me.

Before I had left his office, I told my attorney, "At this point, they gonna have to get a public defender because I will not help them with anything else. So, unless they want to pay you a retainer or something to keep you, you no longer represent them. I'll only be paying for myself."

He told me that was a wise decision and the one he had hoped I would make.

"That is what is damaging. Even if you wanted to go to a trial, they don't really have any evidence on you because all they have is now is hearsay," he said.

The other people, my co-defendants, weren't talking – except for the lady that got caught. The rest of those people were solid.

He said, "You were sleeping with the enemy literally. That relationship of yall's could damage us when going to court."

I was crushed as I thought back on it in my bedroom the next day. I called my friend, Sherry, and a few other friends of mine and told them to come over. I didn't want to tell them over the phone what was happening. I just told them I had something I needed to tell them, and it was very important.

"I need you present and in my face because this is crazy," I said. "I can't tell you over the phone."

As each person dropped by, I caught them up on this new revelation about Zee. Sherry worked first shift. When she got off work at four o'clock in the afternoon and got back to Akron, she came straight to my house. I told her what happened. She couldn't close her mouth and was speechless. Her eyes were as big as half dollars. Like everyone else I had told (with the exception of my mom), she was caught by surprise.

How long do you think you can keep a secret like that from someone who is paying for you attorney? It was like Zee really thought I would never find out, or at least not until he got on the stand to lie on me.

"I'm paying for you to stab me in my back," I told them about Zee. "I wouldn't even know nothing about nothing if it wasn't for you. And, I'm solid enough not to tell on y'all. They didn't catch me doing nothing. They had caught them red handed. They had them on cameras. They had all kinds of stuff. And I still wouldn't tell."

I felt like, if we're gonna go down, we're all gonna go down together. Yeah, this is your stuff, but if we're gonna ride together, if they find out it's you cause they got you on camera or cause you told on yourself, don't try to put that mess on me. That was why we wanted the motion to discovery in the first place. We wanted to know who the snitches were. Come to find out, you're one and this is your operation.

Within a year, I had lost so many people close to me. I had a lot on me that Zee and Zee's daughter had just compounded it. I lost my sister, my nephew, and my mama is dealing with this stuff with my baby brother and middle brother in jail. So, I switched from first shift to working second shift so my mom could keep my kids at night. She worked first shift.

After the truth about Zee's conspiracy against me came out, it was really a blessing. It threw a monkey wrench in the game. We had to change attorneys and do all kinds of stuff. I also went back and forth to court for a year by myself. They put Zee and her daughter on a separate docket because we no longer had the same lawyer, and they weren't going to court with me anymore. Those two went to court together.

I was still working at Dish Network while I was going to court. Before I found out about the plot, I had gotten hired there and started in my training class. I had a couple people from Canton who started that training class with me that I met. A lot of the people who worked there were from that city. I didn't know anybody who worked there previously. Remember, Canton was like 20 minutes from where I was living.

On the first day of the job training, I guess they hadn't gotten all of the people that were supposed to be starting in my class processed. We literally just sat there, did paperwork, and introduced ourselves. We really did nothing, and they paid us because the rest of the people hadn't gotten a chance to do what they needed to do for them to start the class.

On day two, our class was officially started or real. This tall, buff guy walked in. It was about 15 or 20 of us. We were all in class hungry, ready for them to let us take a break so we could eat our lunch. I had been chewing gum and decided to take it out.

The handsome new guy said, "Can I get a piece of that gum?"

I said, "Um, do I know you?"

He was like, "Nah, but I can get to know you."

I busted out laughing. Me and a girl named Dee-Dee that was in my class both laughed at the sexy flirt. Dee-Dee and I became really cool. We met on day one and cliqued. We had the same kind of personality – both of us were outgoing, funny and goofy – and we looked alike. People on the job used to ask us if we were sisters or related some other way because we favored each other so much.

Well, day number two, when the rest of the class came, that's when I met Monty. He was sexy, buff, flirt I told you about. He and this other gentleman, Brandon, were really the only guys in the training class. All of the rest of the class was ladies. So, after we laughed at Monty's request for gum, I went ahead and gave him a piece. After all, we were all starving.

Monty was sitting behind me in the class. I was sitting in the second row and he was sitting in the fourth row. I passed the pack the gum to the girl that was across from me and she passed it back to him. While our instructor was teaching us about the different screens we needed to know about when a customer wants to upgrade to channels like STARZ or HBO, Monty opened the gum and then balled up the wrapper and hit me with it as he chewed a piece.

That was when he passed my pack of gum back through the same girl between us. We were in class clowning. The class was so boring, so we kept doing stuff to keep ourselves entertained. When we finally got our lunch break, Dee-Dee started trying to play match maker.

"I think Monty likes you," she said.

I was like, "Girl, Monty don't like me. He's just being silly. We were passing the time in class."

The next day, after our class, a lot of the people that already worked there said some people from the job were going straight from work to this sports bar. They had planned to do some karaoke, pool and stuff like that before heading home. I knew my kids were going to be spending the night with my mom because we didn't get off work until close to midnight anyway. So, I told them I would go with them.

At this point, I was just working and going home, working and going home. I was still distraught about this whole thing with Zee. I went out with them and had fun because I missed my brothers. I would tell them about my life and what's going on with me. We'd talk about what was going on with my mom and what the kids were up to at that time. I always tried to be strong for my brothers. But my schedule was emotionally and physically draining

My friends could tell when I had left from visiting my brothers in prison. It took a lot out of me to leave there without them with me. Yes, I knew I had to leave them there and they couldn't go with me. But, I saw how they were being treated. I saw how the guards would talk to them. I saw how people abused their authority. I saw how the correctional officers and wardens would just throw inmates in a hole for petty stuff.

I got a chance to see that and I got a chance to see how you have to be violated just to go in to visit your loved ones. You get looked at with suspicion or condemnation. You are spoken to roughly by most, or in a dismissive manner in general. You have to strip naked. You have to bend over and cough. You have to go through all this humiliating stuff just to be able to see your family. So, it was emotional for me every time I went.

One particular day after work when we went to the sports bar, Dee-Dee's husband joined us. He didn't work with us. Well, I was telling them about the situations I was juggling. I told them about my going back and forth to court and all of that. That was another reason why I had changed from the morning shift to work from four until midnight. I could go to court in the morning and won't have to miss work and take money out of my kids' pockets.

"Plus, my mom was working first shift so that way I can be with them during the day. She would be with them at night so they could get into bed, do their work for school, and all of that kind of stuff," I told Dee-Dee.

We had a ball that night. We did karaoke. I got up there and showed a little skilled and clowned around. We did all kinds of stuff at the sports bar that night. Then, Monty and I exchanged telephone numbers.

"I want to call you some time. I want to hang out," he said.

At this point, I didn't know how old he was. He looked older than me, but he looked and acted younger. Plus, like I said, he was a sexy, buff, handsome man. So, he asked to exchange numbers and we did. We went out and hung out. We started talking before work and after work. One day, his car broke down and he was waiting on the tow truck by the side of the road. He asked me if I was working that day. I told him I would be.

"Do you think that, if I give you some gas money, you can pick me up on your way to work so I won't miss work?" He asked. "I can have my mom pick me up after work cause I don't know what's going on with my car."

So, I was like, "Yeah, I'll come get you. I'll just leave home early enough to where I could pick you up and we can both be on time."

I got ready, left home, picked him up, and we went to work. Our lunch breaks were scheduled at different times. The company did this because they wanted to always have somebody to be on the phone. Everyone had noticed from day two of class, the first day Monty showed up, that we had a connection of some sort.

That day I gave him a ride to work, our supervisor said, "Since Tiffany is Monty's boo, we're going to let them go to lunch together."

They were funny like that in the office. Mind you, I wasn't talking to Monty. I wasn't in a relationship with him. I liked him, and everybody kept telling me he liked me, but we were not an item. I guess they thought we were because we rode in to work together a lot for like two months. I remember it took a while before he was able to get his car fixed. I think his engine had gone out. Between me, his mom, Dee-Dee and a couple of other people from work who lived near him, Monty was able to get to work without a problem

170

because several of them lived near him. That one particular day we went to lunch together, he started being funny.

"You know they said you my boo," he said.

I said, "Are you telling these people that?"

He was like, "I ain't telling these people nothing. They must assume that because they would see me riding to work with you."

We also took breaks at the same time, our restroom and stretch breaks. We were always laughing no matter what was going on, and he was always flirting with me or being sarcastic with me. They assumed we had been messing around. All we had done was talked.

That day, we talked on the phone and stuff like that after work. I told hm how I wound up out there, why I had to get the job, and everything else that had happened in my life major up to that point. Everything was an open book. He was telling me some things that was going on in his life too. He told me he had just recently gotten a divorce and he had kids. He told me they were all grown. He started telling me their ages.

I was like, "Wow! How old are you?"

He was 13 years older than me too. He and Zee were born the same year. Zee was born in January of '67 and Monty was born in September '67. I would have never thought he was that old because of the way he acted. He and his son got along more like brothers instead of like father and son. And, he was in excellent shape. He was running around, playing basketball with the guys, running out there with them young guys playing football. I mean, he was rough. I was 26 and he was 39. He was getting ready to be 40. He was in tip-top shape. He was big on health. He worked out every day. I would have never known he was in he was almost 40.

This day, we all go out and then everybody goes back to my house. They drove the 20 minutes from Canton to my house in Akron after we left the sports bar. When we got to my place, we had bottles and went inside to finish having fun. My friend Dee-Dee, her husband, two guys from the job and their fiancés, Monty, Brian and his girlfriend all came back to my place. We were kicking it, playing spin the bottle, listening to music, and doing all kinds of silly stuff just having fun. We looked up and it was three o'clock in the morning.

Everybody was saying they had to get on back to Canton. Their kids were had to go to school the next day and they had to get them ready. My kids were at my mom's house. Other people had to go to school during the day before they went to work in the evening. They didn't anticipate being out that late.

"Well, we're gonna stay for about 15 more minutes and then we're gonna be out," Dee-Dee said.

They offered Monty a ride back to Canton with them and he declined.

"Un un, I'm good."

I was looking at him like, *You is? I'm not driving back, then okay.* Not at no three o'clock in the morning, and then I got to come back and be in this house by myself. That's what we were not gone do. And, one thing about Dee-Dee is she don't bite her tongue about nothing. She will say what's on her mind. She has absolutely no filter.

She said, "Oh, he might be getting ready to make it official tonight."

We all just started laughing.

I said, "Girl, you better get him and take him with you."

She went, "He said he was good. Hey, Monty. You good?"

He was like, "Man, y'all trippin. I'm good. If I have to have somebody come get me, I'm good."

Dee-Dee's husband said, "But we going back to Canton. You can ride with us, man, no problem."

Monty said, "Cool, I'm good though."

Dee-Dee said, "Well, we got to get on home. We got five kids to get ready for school in the morning. We outta here."

They went on and left. Monty and I sat there, still drinking and talking. I was like, *Man, I can't believe this. I don't know what's going to happen when I go to this court.* Instead of staying in my own head, I went ahead and let Monty know what I was thinking.

"I can't leave my kids with my mama," I said. "She got enough on her taking care of my nephew. I'm trying to think of a plan."

Monty started giving me encouragement.

"You know what? I can do what I can to help you and other things will come through. It's gonna work out. It's all gonna work out," he said. "Your kids is not going to be just out there. I don't think you're going to jail. I don't believe they'll give you no eight years for your first time getting in trouble. I just think that they'll probably just give you probation. I know I ain't no lawyer, but I'm just saying what I think."

I appreciated his words. I looked at the time and saw that it was close to 4:30 a.m. So, I piggybacked on that conversation he had with Dee-Dee and her husband before they left.

"How you getting home? I thought you said you could have somebody to come and get you," I mentioned.

Monty was like, "No, I'm staying here with you."

So, you already know what happened from there. We were inseparable from that moment. Then, it became every night that he was coming to my house. But, one day he didn't show up at work. They asked me where he was, and I told them I didn't know. They said he didn't answer his phone when they called him, and they asked me to call him. He didn't answer my call either. So, I called his mom's house.

I was like, "Is Monty okay? Is everything alright. You know what's going on with him? He didn't show up to work and they're asking me where he at and I don't know. I couldn't tell them nothing because I couldn't get him to answer his phone," I told her.

"He had to go to the emergency because he was having chest pains," she said.

So, I went back to the people on the job and told them I had spoken to his mother. I told them what she said was going on with Monty.

"He is having chest pains. He has been in the emergency room all day. That's why he didn't show up to work and that's why he ain't call, because he was actually in the hospital," I said.

They let it slide with that. They let him sign in the following day when he came back to work. I still had to go to court. He came and stayed at my house. He was going back and forth to court with me every month. Sometimes, I had to go once a month. Other times, I had to go twice a month. It all depended on what I was going to court for that particular day.

CHAPTER 16
The Brief Addition

So, Monty and I were in a full-blown relationship. We got off work one day and went to my house as usual. It was round two o'clock in the morning, after we had gone to bed, his cell phone started ringing. I was pissed because, one thing about me when I'm sleeping, nobody better wake me up if it ain't no dire emergency. I was heated.

"Why didn't you put your phone on silent, man? It's already bad enough and hard for me to sleep. Now that I'm asleep, I don't want nobody's phone waking me up," I said.

The call went to voicemail and Monty put the phone on vibrate. His phone kept blowing up. I really to mad then. You know how that vibration sounds. When you want silence, that humming sound seems just as bad as hearing the ringtone.

I was like, "Answer this phone!"

He didn't. So, I picked it up on the next ring.

"Hello!"

It was just silence on the other end. All I heard was dead air. I said it again.

"Hello."

Then, finally, she was like, "Hello."

I said, "Hello."

And, she was like, "I think I called the wrong number."

I said, "Okay."

We hung up the phone. About 10 minutes later, Monty's phone rang again. The same number was on the screen. No name was showing. Still, I recognized it as the same number that had been calling back to back before. I answered it again. Monty was still beside me in bed paying close attention.

I was like, "Hello."

She said, "Okay, maybe I don't quite have the wrong number. Is this Monty's number?"

I said, "Ah, yeah."

She told me her name and I said okay. Then, she asked me my name. I told her my first name.

"Who are you?" She asked.

I said, "Well, the question would be who are you because you're calling at two o'clock in the morning and I'm answering the phone."

She told me she was his girlfriend. I told her I was too and that he lived with me.

"What?" She acted astonished.

I said, "Ah, yeah. Otherwise, why would I be answering his phone at two and three o'clock in the morning."

So, she was like, "Where is he?"

I said, "Right here in the bed next to me, where he's supposed to be, going to sleep. Ma'am, please don't try to come for me, especially with all I'm dealing with. You don't want it."

She was like, "Well, um, my question is, so he stay with you?"

I said, "Again, we are in a relationship and we live together. We have been together pretty much all day every day for the last few months. My question for you is, when do you see him because he's here every day and every night?"

She said, "Well, I was locked up and I just got out of Marysville. I just came home."

I went, "Oh, okay."

She said, "Yeah. That's why I was calling him. I wanted to let him know I was back home. I gotta say, I never heard your name before. I never knew anything about you. You know what I'm saying?"

I replied, "I never knew anything about you or anything with y'all, so what's going on? Better yet, I want to have a conversation with him because my issue was not with you. My issue is with him. As a matter of fact, hold on. Wait right here."

I called his name. He was knocked out now. I shook him and called his name again.

"Monty! Monty! Get up and get up right now," I demanded.

"What's wrong baby?" He asked, rolling over.

"What's wrong is what's going on," I said. "So, you got a girlfriend."

He sat up, "What are you talking about?"

I said, "Your girlfriend is on the phone," and I put the phone on speaker so we all could hear each other.

"It's three o'clock in the morning. She had been calling your phone and she thought she had the wrong number when I answered. But, now she's realized this is your number."

Monty didn't have that same phone before she went in. He had gotten that number after she went to jail. The woman had called his mama's house and his mama gave her his phone number.

"What girlfriend?" He said.

And she spoke up and said, "Hello, Mr. Wellford."

He didn't realize I was on the call with her at that very moment. Nor did he realize that she was on speaker. He woke up all the way then.

"What's up?" He greeted.

She was like, "That's what I'm trying to figure out. I'm trying to figure out what's up. I called your mother's house yesterday when I first got home, but I didn't get nobody until late tonight."

She must have been calling while Monty's mother at work. I guess she kept calling until later that night and finally got her on the phone and she gave the woman his cell phone number.

"She told me you weren't there, and she gave me your number. I just thought, um," the lady said. "See, I was just on the phone with Tiffany and Tiffany is saying that y'all are in a relationship. So, I'm just trying to find out what's up."

Now, I'm sitting there doing the same thing at four o'clock in the morning. Trying to see what the deal is. I was looking at him. He was looking at me. This lady was on the phone waiting for him to answer, and he was silent for a second. Then, basically, he spoke up and told her the same thing I had told her.

"Yeah, I been seeing her for some months now," he said.

I already knew what he and I were doing. I wanted to get to the bottom of what it is that he was supposed to be having with her. That was what I questioned in that moment.

I said, "Well, you never shared with me that you were in a relationship with nobody though."

He was like, "Right before she went away, we were not together. When she ended up going away, I didn't know how long she was even going to be gone away."

So, I was like, *Was they together and he just left her for dead? Was they not together? What is going on?*

She said, "So, you wasn't with me when I left?"

He said, "Naw."

They got to arguing. He grabbed the phone and hung up on her. She called back. They argued some more, and he hung up again. She kept calling back.

I said, "Look, check this out. In the morning, I'm going to take you back to your mama's house. See, what we not gone do is drama. I have enough of that going on in my personal life already. I don't want to get any more unnecessary drama in my life."

He was begging and pleading. He tried his best to get me to change my mind.

"No. Tiffany, I want to be with you. I love you," he said. "You know I love you. I want to be with you. We gonna do this. We gonna do all kinds of things together."

This was the first time I heard that one. Like I said, I was a complete grinder and go-getter.

So, he was like, "We gonna do this, we gonna be together. I wasn't with her when she left. I don't want to be with her. I want to be with you."

I said, "Well, I still need to think over this. So, in the morning I am going to take you to your mom."

We laid on down and got a few hours of sleep. When we got up at nine o'clock that morning, we started getting ready to go. I cooked breakfast as usual and we chatted, but things were a little different. I took him on to Canton and dropped him off at his mother's house before I went back to Akron. We didn't have to work the next day, so I went on about handling business and running errands while I could. Monty kept calling me all day long.

"I don't want you to be mad at me. I don't want us to not be together," he said. "I want us to be together and I want to be there for you. I want you to do great things and I want to do big things with you,"

I was like, "Okay. I see. But, what I'm not gone do is I'm not going to be getting into it with no females. I'm not doing that."

So, he was like, "No, she ain't got no reason to be mad. We was not together when she left. I don't care what she say. I know we was not together and we ain't together now. Will you come pick me up later on?"

I told him, "Yeah. I got some running around to do first. I'm up here now, and then I'll call you around 10 when I'm done."

When I got done with my running around, I stuck to my word. I called Monty because I was going to come pick him up. I finished early though and called his mom's house around six.

I was like, "Monty there?"

She was like, "Naw, he ain't here."

That's when I asked, "You know where he went?"

I caught her off guard. She started stuttering.

"Now, now, now. I don't know wh-where he went. He ain't here," she said.

I was like, *Wow! He must think I'm stupid and the mama must think I'm a dummy.* What I did was blocked my number and called the phone the girl had called from. Neither one of them knew I had gotten her number out of his phone. When I called and she answered, I could hear him talking in the background. I hung up.

When it came time that night for me to pick him up, I told him I had caught a flat tire and I couldn't come because the people wouldn't be able to make it to fix my tire because all the tire places were closed. He said okay.

"That's cool. I'll just see you tomorrow when you come and get me for work. I'll call you a little bit later then since you not gone come tonight," he told me.

Now, this shows you how dumb he was. I had two vehicles at the time. Now he should've known there was another car at my house. Not smart! This is what I did. I waited until 10 o'clock and I pulled up at his mama's house. I went and knocked on the door. His mom opened the door and looked like a deer in headlights.

I said, "Is Monty in?"

She was like, "Um, nope."

I said, "Why is he not here? He knew I was gonna come pick him up at ten o'clock."

She said, "I don't know."

I said, "I had told him I wasn't coming because I had a flat. I'll just go ahead and go."

She closed the door and immediately called out to Monty. I could hear her talking to him through the door.

"Do you know Tiffany just came and knocked on the door?" She asked.

He said, "What?'"

She went, "Yeah. Tiffany. She just came and knocked on the door. And, you're not here."

So, I walked on back to my car as I called his cell phone. I got his voicemail. I thought, *Oh okay, I'm good cause I know he's going to have to think of a lie. Plus, he don't even know that I heard him in the background when I called the girl's phone.* I never said anything to him about it. I'm sure he was thinking, *Oh yeah, I'm going to be Scott free. I'm going to be able to tell her I was asleep, or whatever.* But since his mama done called and told him I showed up at the door, I bet he was in complete disbelief now that he knew I knew he wasn't at home like he said he would be at 10.

The next morning, he called me.

I answered the phone, "What's up? You must have had a ball yesterday."

He said, "What you talkin about?"

That was when I told him, "I already know you was with the lady out of Marysville because I heard your voice in the background when I called her phone yesterday."

He said, "I was just over there talking to her."

I said, "Well, you could have talked to her on the phone. You don't have to be with her to talk to her."

You know what I'm saying?

I said, "You wasn't at your mom's last night when I came because you thought I wasn't coming. I may be younger than you but I ain't no dummy. When you start playing games, don't ever think I'm a fool cause my mama ain't raised a one of them."

He was like, "I was not with her last night!"

I said, "Where were you at then? I find it awfully funny that I didn't even make it off the porch before I heard yo mom call you on the phone, telling you that I was at the front door. When I called you, you didn't answer the phone. But when your mama called you, you picked up right away."

I added, "I don't know what you think this is, but I got too much going on in my personal life. So, you know what I'm gonna do? I'm gonna do you a favor. I'm gonna let you go there and let y'all figure that out."

So, I went to work. I didn't have time for their shenanigans. I went on to work and he got to work how he got there. He was late because he had to get a ride. While we were at work, he came up to me still trying to explain himself.

"I need to talk to you. I don't want to lose you," he said, before adding, "This is what happened,. This is why I had to talk to her."

And this, that and the third.

I said, "Monty, check this out. I got so much going on in my life right now. I couldn't give a damn about you and this mess, or anybody that looked like you and her and this mess. I feel like I am in a battle for my life right now. I have real-life stuff going on and this with y'all doesn't qualify."

I didn't know if I was going to get eight years in prison or if, because each count held different years, the judge could do whatever she wanted with my sentencing. She could decide to run the time together or run it separately if I had to go to prison. There was no way for me to know what the judge's decision would be.

"This kind of stuff is definitely a turn off to me," I told Monty.

So, to try to make me feel better, when I say he came to my house and I couldn't move without him there, that was not an understatement. I couldn't go to the bathroom by myself. He came and stayed at my house and did not leave. He packed his things from his mama's house and brought them to my house. We went back and forth to court for my case.

After the lady called and I found out about them being recovering drug addicts, that's where the codependency came from. Everything started to get revealed. I wondered what she went to prison for and one of my cousins reminded me that it was public information and I could look it up online. So, I went online and started fishing around to find out why Monty's former lover went to Marysville.

One night, Monty left work early. He said an emergency had happened at his mom's house and he needed to leave. He told me to call him when I got off work.

"Babe, call me. I'm gonna have you to come get me," he said.

Well, I got off work and I called him. No answer. I called him again. No answer. By this time, we had been together for about six months. So, I called him all night. I never got him. I went to his mom's house the next morning after I took my kids to school. That was when I found out Monty and Zee had more in common than their birth year. This was how I found out that Monty and Zee were actually the same type of person. The only difference was the abuse.

It was Monty's mom who laid it all out for me in greater detail. She said her son had been dabbling with various addictions for a long time. She said that was how he got involved with that lady who has returned.

"I really didn't want to give her the number, but she kept calling on the phone. She left so many messages. I went ahead and answered her. That wasn't for me to decide if he talks to her again or not," she said.

After his mama ran the whole story down to me, I understood why Monty wasn't answering the phone the night before nor that day.

"He's probably not answering the phone because he's probably on one of his binges," she said.

I was floored! This seemed impossible to me. When I say Monty was buff, he could be a bodybuilder. I mean, he was really in shape and healthy, all this stuff. He was always fresh and was so even tempered and seemingly straight-laced. *They are the same people. I am attracting the same person with the same birth year and the same characteristics.*

But, can you guess who else they had the same characteristics of? My father. My dad was on and off drugs, in and out of jail and prison, and smoother than satin. The only thing that Monty did right, bless his heart, was he never went behind bars – even though he'd been in a bunch of stuff that could've gotten him there. God spared him from that.

Even TD was like my dad in a way. He went to jail a few times, sold drugs but never was on drugs. He was way older than me. Some of the same characteristics as my father. When I met TD, he had that dealer lifestyle like my father before he was even sent to jail for the first time. By the time we split, he had been in and out a few times, and afterwards I heard he returned a few more times.

Like back then, I was still looking for that figure. You see what I'm saying? So, when Monty's mom shared with me the details she did about his past with drug addiction, I felt like somebody had kicked me in the stomach and knocked the wind out of me. She kept talking to me. She was saying a lot of stuff. But I really couldn't even hear her. It was like a tank had run me over. All I could think was, *This cannot be happening to me again. This cannot be life?*

She knocked the wind out of me. Two days later, he showed back up at her house. She called me from her job and told me about it. I guess she didn't want anyone at her job to hear her talking.

"He showed up this morning," she told me in a rushed whisper.

So, when he came back to work, he could tell I knew what he had been doing and I could tell he was embarrassed. Even though no one on the job knew about his binge, we knew. I was giving him looks like, *This cannot be for real.* It got to where I couldn't do my job right because I was so taken aback. *I can't believe my life is going in a complete circle.* I was talking to the people and quoting the wrong prices. It was like my head just was not in the game.

It couldn't help but be noticed. They had people whose sole job it was to monitor the phones. One of the shift managers came to my desk and asked me to come to the office when I finished my current call. They wanted to have a talk with me about the call I had completed previously.

"Is everything okay?" The shift lead asked.

"We've noticed that you're not yourself today," the floor manager said. "Where are you getting this information you're giving out? It's all wrong."

I was like, "I'm sorry. I don't even know what I said. I need my sheet I guess. I'm really under a lot of stress."

So, they wound up letting me leave work early that day. Monty was blowing my phone up. He kept calling me and calling me. When I answered the phone, he started his bid.

"I need to talk to you. I need to tell you my side. I need to tell you my side."

So, that evening when he texted me, I still didn't respond. Finally, he called me from his mom's house number. I was thinking it was her and I answered. It was him.

He was like, "Please, don't hang up. Let me explain. Just give me five minutes, please don't hang up. I really want to talk to

189

you in person because I don't feel like this is something that we should talk about over the phone. My mom told me the things she shared with you about me and, um, I think you have the right to know, but I want you to hear what I need to say for me."

So, I responded, "I'll think about it."

He was like, "No, really. For real. Even if you never talked to me again after this, I need to tell you my side."

I said, "Well, I gotta get my kids, but okay. I'll come talk to you."

He requested, "Just come get me from my mama's house. I don't even want to be here. I just want to go somewhere neutral, the park or wherever there's nobody else around. I just want to talk to you myself."

I told him okay. There was a park down the street from his mother's house. I went to Canton and picked him up from her house and we went to the park and sat at a picnic table. That was when he just started spilling his guts. He was basically telling me details to some of the things he had touched on in the beginning. Then, he dropped things on me that were complete surprises.

Monty has been in the military and was once stationed in Alaska. He and some of his fellow enlistees were smoking and, I guess, one of the guys that they smoked with had laced the weed. They were smoking primos. After he got out of the military, it was all downhill from there for him.

He told me, "I don't want to do this. I've been battling this on and off for many years."

He said, after he got out of the military, he was clean for a long time. Then, something tragic happened in his life and it sent him seeking out cocaine. Basically, it was something dealing with his relationship with his father. His father lived in Texas Monty went to Texas with the hopes of trying to build a relationship with him. I guess the rejection sent him on a downward spiral.

He was like, "I've been trying to get myself back on track, really, since then and that's how I wound up at my mom's. That's why I am here. And you know, uh, going through stuff with my ex-wife triggered me so I moved back in with my mother and said I was gonna rebuild my life. That's how I met the girl that called. She wasn't even really my girlfriend. She was just somebody that I was messing around with and we both was in the same lifestyle. We were not together and when she left."

It now made sense to me why she would think they were a couple and he would be adamant that they weren't. I believed being back in communication with her triggered him to go back to that life. Because, with them being so together in it, they will always be each other's triggers back to that world. She was his trigger, she was back, and I believed he was back too.

He said, "That's why I was telling you I wanted to meet with her. I want to tell her that, since she's been gone, my life has been different. That's why I was so good with being there with you. Our relationship was something that I never had. Even me being married, I didn't have that. My wife wasn't even supportive of me and I was her supporter."

Monty was venting, "You know, what we had those months was something that I never had with no woman before. When I found out how old you were , I couldn't believe it because you were so polished for your age. I have a daughter around your age. I couldn't believe how much older you seemed. You didn't act like a typical 26-year-old woman. I want you to know that I want to get help and I want to live a productive life. I just never knew how to do it. My mother is my biggest example of how to be better. I love my mom, but she's always been my crutch. That's why, when we started being together and hanging together, I never would really drink alcohol."

I believed him. I had noticed, even though when we went to my house that night and everybody was drinking, he drank only a little while we all indulged. I mean, we were kicking it, throwing back bottles. He wasn't doing that. He was just chilling.

"I already know that could trigger me to go out there. So, I didn't do that," he said. "I had one drink with y'all and that was good for me. But, I really do want help. I really do want it to work. I really do want this relationship with you."

He told me what his dreams were for his life and the things he wanted still to provide for his children, although they were grown. He told me he wanted to own his own business. He wanted to own some houses. He really wanted to do something with himself. And I, at the time, I believed him fully while another part of me doubted his words and intentions towards me just as much.

I was like, "I don't know. You're telling me what you want me to hear? Or, are you really telling me what you want to do?"

So, Monty came and stayed with me for the second time around. Then, before long, it was time for me to go to court again. He made it a point to be there with me that time too. I was happy to have it back to being just him and me.

CHAPTER 17
Kept In The Loop

When we got to court, my attorney pulled us to the side to drop a bug in my ear. He said we would be coming back to court in two weeks and that I will either have to enter a plea or demand a trial.

You already know, the plea wasn't really a deal and I wasn't going for that. Everyone knew the only "deal" was that the prosecutor on my case was actually from Canton (the same place in Stark County my lawyer was from and not from Summit County where I lived) and she was trying to make a name for herself. She was a brand-new prosecutor trying to sensationalize and aggrandize my case in hopes of being able to say she sent us each away for a minimum of eight years. Seriously! She never come off eight years.

"Eight years. Eight years! I want her to do eight years," she argued. "These companies have taken these losses, some have gone out of business, and she needs to be held accountable."

Like I said, I never was the person who made the companies the losses. This wasn't my operation. I was just one of the people who got introduced to the operation. But because I wouldn't snitch, it made me look like it was me spearheading the whole operation. It was after all that when my attorney told me the options I now had.

"Next week, we're gonna either have to take a plea deal or we want to change your plea from not guilty to guilty before taking it to trial to let the judge decide your sentencing," he said. "But let me tell you what you have in your favor. One, your judge is a Christian. Two, you have the judge who every person getting in trouble wishes they had. She is the most compassionate person that I know. As far as judges now at the Summit County Courthouse, Judge Eleanor Stormer is the most compassionate. But, those are our two options."

Time we finished, I talked to Monty. Everything had started getting real for me, like for real. Now, we were down to crunch time. I had been going to court for the last year and basically having this relationship with him for a whole year. I met him right after I started that job. We had been dating for almost a year now. It was in this moment after that the hearing that the real questions started.

"What if I do go to prison? If I go to prison, where are you gonna be? What are you gonna do? Are you going to be there for me? Are you going to disappear? What, what are you going to do?" I asked bluntly.

He said, "I'm going to be there for you. I'm going to be willing to do whatever. You're not going to be in this alone. You are not in it alone right now."

So, before it was time for me to go back to court. I kept feeling really bad. I think I was making myself sick because of my nerves. I was feeling ill. I was feeling sick.

I said, "Monty, I'm gonna need you to take me to the doctor's office. I'm gonna call my doctor and make me an appointment, but I want you to take me because I keep feeling like I am dizzy, and I don't want to drive like this."

He said, "Okay."

I told Monty, "This is my blood sugar and me being stressed out about this stuff. I know I gotta change my plea and I need to go sit down and talk to my momma to figure out what the plan's gonna to be if I go to prison. We got to come up with a solution for my kids, and we need to be figuring that stuff out now."

Monty agreed. When the day of my appointment rolled around, I went to the doctor to get myself checked out. They told me I had the flu, was dehydrated, and my blood pressure was up high. They gave me the shots, pills and prescriptions they normally give for the flu. They also gave me some fluids and told me to be sure to drink plenty over the next few days. Once the prescription for the blood pressure pills and other medication was filled, Monty picked them up for me and we went on home.

With everything going on in my everyday life, I didn't realize I hadn't even had my cycle. I was like, *Oh my, God. My cycle. Dang! I ain't even had no cycle. This is crazy.* I knew the stress I had been under, and I rationalized that it was definitely enough to throw anyone's cycle off. So, I called my cousin and was talking to her on the phone about all the pressure I was under. As always, she was giving me words of encouragement.

"I'm praying for you. You know, God don't make mistakes," Tasha said.

And I was like, "Girl, can you believe I didn't even have my cycle? I think I done stressed myself out so bad that I can't even have my cycle."

She said, "Girl, you gotta be making sure that's just stress."

I told her, "No, Tasha. I don't think it's nothing like that. I just think I've been stressed out. I had the flu and all of this other stuff happening too."

She laughed, "Okay, 'I had the flu.'"

She was making me think then.

"Just get a pregnancy test just to be on the safe side," Tasha urged. "Just go ahead, take the pregnancy test, and see what it says."

I tried to tell her that wasn't the case again.

"Girl, I don't need to take no pregnancy test. I'm good. Look, all this stuff has had me stressed out. I even just went to the doctor and they told me I had the flu and was dehydrated. They even gave me fluids and a prescription for my blood pressure because it was up and that was why I was feeling dizzy. I don't need no pregnancy test. You know how I be when I get pregnant. I don't believe it's that."

Because my blood pressure was so high during that visit, I was scheduled to go back for them to recheck my blood pressure to see how I was doing on the medication. When I went back to the doctor's office, I saw the physician who had been my family doctor forever and told him about everything I'd been feeling. He already knew what I was going through. And when I told him my cycle had not come and I believed it was because of all the stress, he started talking like Tasha.

"Well, let's just be on the safe side," he said. "I'll do you a pregnancy test. And, um, I want to monitor your blood pressure. Every week, I want you to come in and get a blood pressure check."

I told him I would. Then he checked me out, checked my blood pressure, and I peed in the cup and left. About an hour later, as I'm almost nearing my house after running a few other errands, my phone rang, and it was the doctor's office calling me.

"Where did you go? You left?" The shocked nurse inquired.

I told her, "Yes. He said I was done. All I was getting was a blood pressure check."

She asked, "Did he have you to pee in a cup?"

I told her, "Yeah. I left my pee in the chair."

She said, "I know. That's what I'm calling you about. You're pregnant."

I said, "What?"

She said, "You're pregnant."

I immediately pulled my car over. Reception on these cell phones plays tricks, we know. I posed my question to the nurse again.

"What?"

She said, "Okay. We are going to try this again. You are pregnant."

It was straight silence at that point. It was clear and it was a wrap. Monty was at the house because we had to go to work, and I was just going to go get a blood pressure check to make sure my medication was working properly. Since the nurse ended up telling me I needed to return to their office for a prescription for prenatal vitamins, I knew I would have to tell him in the next few minutes when I saw him. How else would I explain my need to get back by the doctor's office on the way to work? *This can't be real life. This really can't be, not right now.*

"And, we will have to monitor you because you're definitely going to be high risk being that you're an insulin-dependent diabetic," the nurse made a point to mention.

I just could not fathom a pregnancy happening right then. I couldn't help but express that to the nurse.

"Are you telling me I'm pregnant? I don't even know what I'm getting ready to go to prison for eight years or not," I said in a panic.

To try to relieve a little pressure off me, knowing I was almost home and had to go to work, the nurse gave me another option.

"I can just send the prescription over to your pharmacy. But if you need proof of pregnancy for family services or anything, I can just write it for you, and you can just stop by the office and get it."

That piece of paper proving pregnancy would have made the drive back for the prescription and the rush to work worth it.

"As a matter of fact, I've already turned around to come back and pick that up," I told her.

You know me. I'm a visual person. Even though I'm in a state of shock, I need to see this on a piece of paper. So, I turned around and, after about eight minutes, pulled into a parking spot at the doctor's office.

"I'm preparing the paperwork now," the nurse said as she saw me walk in.

She asked me when I had my last menstrual cycle. They calculated that my baby was initially supposed to be born on August 7, 2007. *This can't be for real*, I kept saying to myself. The nurse handed me the paper with the due date on it and she just went ahead and gave me the prescription for the prenatal vitamins.

"Call the OB/GYN and make an appointment to be seen ASAP since this is a high-risk pregnancy because you're diabetic," she instructed.

I did that. The following week was when I was supposed to go to court to change my plea or cop one. Well, my attorney called me and said that the judge called for a continuance because she had some health issues going on and needed to move back her docket two more weeks.

"That's cool. That gives me a little bit more time," I said.

Thankfully, it ended up being a month later that we were to appear again.

CHAPTER 18
A Whole New Chapter

As I got closer to the house that afternoon, I figured Monty should be getting ready for work by now. When I walked in, I saw he was.

"How was the blood pressure?" He asked me time I walked inside the house.

"It was great. It was good," I said.

"Why are you saying like that?" He probed.

I was like, "No. It was good. I need to talk to you about something really serious."

He fastened his belt as he said, "Okay. What?"

I handed him the piece of paper the nurse at the doctor's office gave me just minutes prior. He sat on the sofa.

"Is this for real?" He asked, still looking at the paper.

"Well, um, this is definitely not for fake," I said. "What am I supposed to do if I'm going to prison? I don't want to have my baby in prison. I don't want to do this."

I was flooded with emotions. I was about to let them all pour out. Then, I caught myself. I didn't want to drown him in my misery. I didn't even want me to keep drowning. All I could do cry. All my anxieties ganged up on me and threw combos as all my feelings rushed in. *What am I going to do about having a baby*

202

knowing next month I have to go change my plea to guilty so some judge can decide my fate? I know I didn't do nothing to deserve to get no eight years. I need to clear my name and be here for my kids!

Monty stayed there by my side. The time came for court and I was still going back and forth to the doctor. Thankfully, they were saying my baby was healthy although my pregnancy was still high risk. Now, I had to go to the doctor every two weeks, like a regular pregnant woman would at the end of her pregnancy. The day before I was supposed to go to court to change my plea, I went to the doctor's office and they reminded me that I would still need extensive care and intensive monitoring because of the health issues I had going on.

At the courthouse the next day, some of everybody was there – including the most important people in my life who were there to support me. Monty was there. My mom was there. I had some friends there. Of course, my kids were not there and my brothers (both still incarcerated) weren't able to be present. Still, I felt their love and support cradling me close as the judge addressed me.

"Did you want to take the plea deal, or would you like to change your plea from not guilty to guilty?" She asked.

She read to me what the charges were, and she told me what potential sentencing they each could carry. She told me If I changed my plea to guilty, she would give me an opportunity to explain myself and let her know why I feel whatever I feel before her sentencing. I went ahead and told the judge I wanted to change my plea from not guilty to guilty.

"Why should I not send you to prison?" She asked. "Now, before you say what you're about to say, I want you to think hard because I also have feedback from the police and detective who say you were not cooperating with them."

Everybody connected to the case was in court that day. From the big financial institutions to the big chain stores whose names we all know well, no one critical to the case was absent. Representatives for some of every entity were sitting there. When they took the stand, they sternly said why they felt like I should go to prison. I presented the proof of pregnancy paper I had with me and spoke candidly to the judge to be sure she knew I was being sincere and honest.

"Your honor," I began, "it wasn't that I wasn't cooperative with them. It's just that I felt like if they caught me doing something or they wanted to question me about something, he should question me about what I did and not what other people did. We live in a society today where you can't go around dropping names and saying things about people because your safety and your family's safety could be at risk. You never know. Even if my safety was not at risk, I feel like that's their job to figure out what happened and how it happened. My job is to answer questions they ask me about me.

"If that's being uncooperative, then I am guilty of that. I'm guilty of not cooperating because I don't feel like it's my duty to tell anything about anybody that has been implicated except myself. I can't tell you nothing about what you say somebody else did. I can only tell you about what I know Tiffany did. Whatever anybody else did has nothing to do with me. I'm standing before you to ask the court for leniency. For one, I just found out that I'm pregnant and my pregnancy is high risk due to the fact that I'm an insulin dependent diabetic. I have some other health issues going on too, and I know that I would not get the proper care I need in prison. Another reason I ask for leniency is because my mother is not in the best of health. She already has my brother's son and I did not want to burden her with caring and providing for my two children and now a third child. Physically, I don't feel like she'll be able to do that."

I continued, "But anything that I'm pleading guilty to was not done to be malicious. It was not done to hurt anybody. It was all out of me trying to help others at the time. That's why I did it. Was it wrong? Absolutely. Do I take responsibility? Absolutely. Do I want favoritism? No, but what I do want is for you to see me as a person and not what they've made me look like on paper. I'm not an animal. I'm not, regardless of what people may think, going around robbing people or hurting anybody or anything like that.

"So, I ask for you to show me mercy. Allow me to be able to still be a mother to my children and to be able to be a daughter to my mother, to help her out like I've been doing. Please, if only for the simple fact that not only does she have serious health issues, but I have health issues going on too."

I made it a point to tell the judge, "I thank you for your consideration," as my final words.

She sat there. The seconds of silence were so loud I could hear my mother screaming in her thoughts. I was telling myself, *Don't worry. Stay calm and quiet. Just keep your head up.*

The judge said, "I just want you to know, you're going to prison."

My heart fell to my stomach and my throat closed up. I heard my mother trying to contain her lament.

"You're going to prison because you should've cooperated with the police. You should have thought about what you were saying when you told him that you wouldn't cooperate with them. I'm gonna tell you another reason why I'm sending you to prison," she said. "I'm not sending you to prison because I believe that you're a bad person. I'm not sending you to prison to even punish you. I'm sending you to prison because I want you to learn a life lesson. I believe that you are a good individual that made a bad choice. I believe that you're a good individual that got caught up with the wrong people. And, I believe that you are the scapegoat. That's why I'm not going to give you eight years in prison, like you robbed somebody when you didn't. And, I'll make you eligible to file for judicial release as soon as six months from now. But, you are going to prison."

My mother just busted out crying. Her wail could probably be heard for miles. She was crying, hollering, screaming and making all kinds of sounds of grief and protest in that courtroom.

The judge said, "Order! Order! This is what I'm going to do. Since you didn't do anything violent and this is your first offense, I'm going to give you 30 days to get your affairs in order. You can get your kids situated so you don't have to uproot them. You can get your finances in order and all of your stuff in order. I want you back here in 30 days. You need to have yourself turned in by 10 o'clock that morning or I am issuing a warrant for your arrest and it's going to be worse."

I walked out the courtroom that day with the opportunity to have 30 days to get my affairs in order. That's just what I did. Since my mother lived in a two-bedroom apartment and I lived in a four-bedroom house, I decided it was best for her to move into my house. I did not want to uproot my kids out of their home because life was already bad enough with their mother getting ready to go to prison. At this time, TD was in prison too.

I told my mom, "You know I have this four-bedroom house. What I'm going to do is pay my rent up for one year. And since she say I got the opportunity to get out on judicial release in six months, hopefully, when I file, they let me out in six months – especially since I've never been in trouble before. This way, my kids ain't gotta get uprooted from their school and daily lives. You can just move in here and it'll be like it's life as usual."

So, we went around and gathered boxes. The next day, we started packing up the stuff in my mom's apartment. By the third day, we were moving her into my house. The kids were so excited to have their grandma moving in with us. I was relieved to know they would all still be taken care of when the time came for me to go away.

EPILOGUE

Monty was around for those 30 more days until it was time for me to go turn myself in. After I turned myself in, I didn't hear from him for about four months. When they took me into custody, I stayed in the county jail after my sentence. I stayed in there for about 10 days. Then, they woke me up one morning.

My mother had come to see, me at the county jail a couple times. She was scheduled for a visit that next day. See, they never tell you when you're riding out because they don't want people to plan anything that can cause a security breach. So, that day they woke me up at four o'clock in the morning.

"Pack it up. We're getting ready to transport you," a correctional officer said.

That's when I got transported to Marysville Correctional Institution for Women. Now, it's called the Ohio Reformatory for Women in Marysville, Ohio. That's where everything got crazy. I was getting ready to start serving my two-year sentence.

I got to Maryville and I was seeing limits to advantages and criminal activity from the door. I saw women being beat by guards. I saw women being taken advantage of sexually by guards. One of my bunkies that slept right across from me had seizures. She wasn't supposed to be on the top bunk. She kept telling them that plus she had a bottom bunk order. One night she had a seizure and fell off the top bunk and died! You see where this was heading?

I was thinking, *I have to go through two years of this in this prison? And I'm Pregnant! Help me, Lord!* That's when it got crazy.

So, you have some more time, I'll get into what happened to me in prison. I'm telling you now, you gotta bring your tissues next time. You will be in tears. You do know that when I was in prison they . . . no, I'll save it for later. You've got to sleep, and I need to rest too.

I had to get this out! I appreciate you more than words can say for your listening ear and for being that shoulder for me to cry on while I told you this first half of my story. This was real therapy for me. Sleep will be good tonight for us all. Come back when you're free again so you can hear the rest of my story. Thank you enormously for this time and the part you played in helping me get **from the pit to the palace**.

If there's one message that I seek to drive home by sharing these real-life experiences with you, it is for you to remember to find the good. Know that, it doesn't matter what you face or have been through, good can come out of any bad situation. You don't have to be a victim. You can be a victor! I want every woman, especially, to know they can defy the odds. Anything you set your mind to, and anything God sets for you, nobody can stop it. It doesn't matter what you've been through. You can come out!

ACKNOWLEDGEMENTS

I extend gratitude to God for the great people always placed along my path.

I thank my husband and my children for always supporting me, encouraging me, and inspiring me.

I thank my parents for preparing me to be the best version of myself.

My gratitude also extends to my siblings, friends, relatives, teachers, spiritual leaders, and business mentors. Having a system of people around like you helps me daily.

And, to you, my readers I give my most gracious thanks. Because you did not "have to" but you did, your support means just as much to me as that of people I've known all my life. Realize that YOU MATTER a lot to me too.

I Thank You!

THE ART & ARTIST

THE BOOK

Published with assistance from BePublished.org in September 2019, **FROM THE PIT TO THE PALACE** is the debut literary release by Tiffany McIntosh and the Texas author's first installment of a two-part series. This true story naming names takes readers through the formative years of a strong life, leaving no life-altering experience unaddressed.

"I wrote this book about my own life to show people that, no matter what you face or have been through, good can come out of any bad situation," the entrepreneur and family woman said. "I want people to know they don't have to be a victim, they can be a victor. You can defy the odds. Anything you put your mind to, with God beside you, you can do it!"

Available as an ebook for $9.95, **FROM THE PIT TO THE PALACE** by Tiffany McIntosh may also be purchased worldwide as a paperback for $22.95 and hardback for $34.95 from bricks-and-mortar and online book retailers including Barnes & Noble, your local bookstore, Borders, TiffanyMcIntosh.webs.com and Amazon.

Tiffany McIntosh, an Ohio native, is a Texas resident and a member of Riverpointe Church in Richmond, Texas. After receiving divine inspiration one day while in a pit of despair, she held in her heart the idea of writing a book and maintained faith that one day she would be in a position to publish it. It was in 2010 that she penned her first words and, despite losing the manuscript, nine years later released **FROM THE PIT TO THE PALACE**.

Born in the small town of Akron, Tiffany was raised by a single mother along with her two younger brothers. She graduated from Firestone High School and attended college at the University of Akron. After leaving college, McIntosh worked a few dead-end jobs until she met someone who introduced her to the industry of network marketing. This is the field and platform through which she eventually met her amazing husband, Calvin McIntosh. The couple has five wonderful children and an awesome grandson.

The founder of the women's empowerment group "6 Figure Chics," Tiffany is dedicated to helping women around the globe know their purpose and to empowering them to be who God called them to be! She is also a six-figure income earner and top leader in her company, with teams in several countries (the largest being in the United Kingdom). The CEO of Paradise Travel LLC, Tiffany is also co-owner of Sacred Kingdom Clothing Company – a Christian clothing line. Her family now resides outside Houston, Texas, but are touching lives globally.

Tiffany's upcoming projects include motivational speaking engagements around the world to help troubled teen girls find their purpose. Tiffany has also started a group for teens. Further, she plans to help thousands of families become financially free by showing them how to own their own travel agency. She said she will travel to other parts of the world to help women in general as well. In what can be considered as her spare time, Tiffany enjoys watching movies, going to amusement parks, playing board games, and traveling. She especially loves spending time with her family.

TiffanyMcIntosh.inteletravel.com

PlannetMarketing.com/1travelqueen

TiffanyMcIntosh.webs.com

6figurechics1.wixsite.com/website

Made in the USA
Columbia, SC
29 August 2020

18347668R00122